BECOME WHAT YOU ARE

Growing in Christian Character

Bishop Julian Porteous

Published in 2012 by Connor Court Publishing Pty Ltd,

Reprinted 2016

Copyright © Bishop Julian Porteous 2012, 2016

ALL RIGHTS RESERVED. This book contains material protected under International and Federal Copyright Laws and Treaties. Any unauthorised reprint or use of this material is prohibited. No part of this book may be reproduced or transmitted in any form or by any means, electronic or mechanical, including photocopying, recording, or by any information storage and retrieval system without express written permission from the publisher.

Connor Court Publishing Pty Ltd
PO Box 7257
Redland Bay QLD 4165
sales@connorcourt.com
www.connorcourt.com

ISBN: 9781925501995 (pbk.)

Cover design by Maria Giordano

Printed in Australia

"Behold the mystery of your salvation laid out for you; behold what you are, become what you receive"
St Augustine of Hippo

CONTENTS

Introduction

What is Character?.. 1

Part 1
Christian Anthropology

1. Made in the Image of God... 15
2. The Question of Good and Evil.. 31
3. In Need of Redemption... 37
4. A Life in the Holy Spirit... 47

Part 2
Christian Character

1. The Pursuit of Virtue.. 53
2. The Disciplined Life – Asceticism.................................... 61
3. A Foundational Virtue – Humility................................... 75
4. The Freedom of Obedience.. 87
5. Personal Integrity – Justice.. 101
6. Chastity – the Guardian of Love..................................... 117
7. The Crowning of the Virtues – Love............................... 139
8. Service – Engagement with the World........................... 149
9. Hope and Joy – the Fruit of Christian Character........... 161

Part 3
Holiness of life

1. Life in God... 169
2. Prayer.. 187
3. Holiness of Life... 203

Conclusion.. 217

Introduction

Human beings are naturally drawn to inquire into the nature of things. The poet, the painter, the musician, seeks to give expression to human experience. The human being has an ability to reflect on experience and to search out the meaning of things. Human beings are seekers. Each person at some time ponders the meaning of their existence and asks the ultimate question: what is the purpose of my life? Human beings are drawn to consider the nature of life: the question is posed - who are we? What makes us what we are? What is our destiny?

While we can speculate about our origins and the meaning of our existence, what is also of importance for each of us is the question of what sort of person we are becoming in life. Our response to the circumstances of our lives shapes us and adds to the creation of the sort of person we are becoming. Each person has certain natural characteristics and our early experiences significantly mould our view of life. We are shaped by what happens to us, but our personal decision-making is a major factor that leads us to develop the sort of person we become. This is what we can call our character. We are in a constant state of becoming a particular type of person.

I would propose that our character becomes our most valuable possession. In the end it is not our possessions or achievements, our popularity or our status that are finally important. Rather it is what sort of person we have become. In other words it is the quality of our character.

The question of the formation of character is a timely one. Our society is undergoing radical change at the personal and social level. There are forces at work that deconstruct the traditional patterns of human life – the family, the understanding of masculinity and femininity, our view on the nature and use of our sexuality. These forces are rebuilding human society in such a way that it is free from the influence of a religious perspective on life and free from the constraints of a moral approach to human living. The modern attitude is to reject traditional models of the virtuous life in favour of a self-realisation freely pursued outside the constraints of moral codes. There is a certain "morality" which is fashioned by society. Certain things are determined to be "politically correct". Certain stances become fashionable like ecological sensitivity or the perceived threat from sexism, but these are fluid positions and change with fashions of thought. They do not impinge particularly on the inner quality of character but rather reflect certain acceptable attitudes. They are superficial and do not promote serious inner growth.

Since the days of the sexual revolution in the mid 1960s there has been a steady eroding of a Christian approach to many life issues – particularly issues concerned with the ethics of human relationships, the role of sexuality in relationships, the sanctity of human life from its conception to natural end, and many issues related to medical ethics (e.g., the use of embryonic stem cells). Living in contemporary society we cannot avoid being affected by these all pervasive social influences which are being actively promoted. Even those who have a basic Christian faith can be hard pressed to accept and live by traditional Christian norms. What is also being affected by these social forces is a reconstruction of the quality of character. The cult of the celebrity, for instance, presents images of personality that are very influential – think of the popularity of celebrity magazines.

There is a need to revisit the question of character from a Christian perspective. This will involve the application of our faith to the question, drawing on the teaching of the Church and the saints in an effort to rebuild an understanding of the true nature of the human person and what constitutes Christian character.

This is the aim of this book. It seeks to explore the nature of the human person. Then, by drawing on our Christian tradition, consider the ways in which we can build a healthy and happy life fulfilling what God has intended us to become as a faithful imitation of his Son. This is a book about identifying the nature of Christian character. It offers a path which will lead to mature Christian character.

What is character?

How can we understand the nature of character? Character is that cluster of values and attitudes which shape our modes of behaviour. Character is what we have become as a result of the myriad of factors that have influenced us and the daily choices we have made. What we are is not so much a chronicle of what we have done or achieved, but rather the way in which our personality has formed. Character cannot be determined by a review of our curriculum vitae, though it may give insight into the pattern of activities that have influenced and formed us. Character is an elusive concept to determine in a person. We identify certain qualities that mark the patterns of thought and behaviour. We notice the way a person responds to situations and other people.

Character is intangible, but it is absolutely real. It is what people readily recognise about us, though we may be slow to see it in ourselves. As humans we quickly sum up our perception of the character of others. It is necessary to assist us in adapting our response to the relationship. We constantly assess the character of others, but often find it difficult to identify its nature in ourselves.

The English word "character" is derived from the Greek *charaktêr* which was originally used as a mark impressed upon a coin. Later the word came to mean a distinctive mark by which one thing was distinguished from others and then primarily to mean the assembly of qualities that distinguish one person from another. In modern usage there is a tendency to merge the words "character" and "personality." While both are sometimes used interchangeably for our purposes we will use the word "character" to refer to the acquired aspects of personality.

The nature of character is not only a descriptive assessment of the qualities of the person but also involves a moral assessment. For example we identify certain qualities as having a significant moral dimension, such as truthfulness. It may be more useful for our purposes to speak of "personality" as referring to the natural dispositions of a person, while we can speak of "character" as a description of the acquired moral qualities of the person. Thus we can say that character is the moral dimension of the personality of a human being and that it reveals itself in the way in which the person conducts his or her life.

Character implies rationality and a moral capacity. In this sense we say that animals do not have character. Character is something always in formation. Character is not just imprinted on us by virtue of the circumstances of our life but it is something which we as rational and moral beings can actively seek to fashion. We can form a view of what sort of person we wish to become and then set out to become that sort of person. We are the agents of what we become.

The character of each human being at any stage of his/her life is the outcome of the complex interplay of a number of elements. While we share a common nature as human beings each person's life is remarkably unique. Each one has a history particular to themselves. It is unrepeatable.

The two particular factors that influence character are the original or inherited elements of a person's being and those qualities that have been acquired. Each human being has a certain nature or disposition which includes a capacity for knowledge, the experience of feelings, and a tendency towards decision and action. This will vary from individual to individual. This raw material for character comes from what is inherited. It forms the person's individuality at the beginning of life and it includes susceptibilities for responding to external influences, and the potential for developing in ways which differ with each human being. Each person has an original capacity and a disposition of mind which determines how experiences will be lived out.

One final point that can be made is that we use the word, "character" in a narrower sense, as when we speak of a person "of character". Here the notion of character implies a certain unified set of qualities which are expressed in consistent modes of behaviour. It is this question of the development of certain defining qualities that mark someone as a person of substance that is the focus of the following chapters.

Individual and corporate character

While we will be focussing on character as developed within individuals, we should also note that there is a corporate mode of character. This is what we often refer to as culture. For instance, in the culture in which I was raised we hear people referring to certain attitudes or behaviours as "un-Australian". This presupposes that there is a cluster of values and attitudes reflected in our national psyche as Australians. We like to think that we as a nation prize certain qualities that distinguish us from other peoples. It is something we celebrate, albeit sometimes in rather crass ways. We like to think that we reflect qualities like a "fair go". We think of ourselves as embodying egalitarianism. This sense of national identity has emerged from our history as a nation. We celebrate our convict past and the rugged conquest of a harsh environment as helping to constitute our national identity. We consider the ANZAC experience in World War I as forging qualities that are now embedded in our national psyche. The harrowing experiences of the First World War fashioned a spirit of mateship and we consider that it is still a quality of high value in our nation. We also like to think of ourselves as maintaining a larrikin spirit that doesn't take everything too seriously. Some popular Australian films, like *The Castle*, capture this spirit.

In addition to the character of a people or nation, various business and social organisations can embody a certain character. Many corporations these days are conscious of how they are perceived by the public. They know that the public attitude towards them can influence their success. Many organisations seek to capture the defining qualities of their corporate personality in mission statements. In a brief statement the organisation seeks to give expression to its distinctive spirit. Advertising produced by the organisation seeks to transmit the spirit of the organisation. Personnel (HR) departments develop programs promoting certain values which they want the employees to reflect. In other words, there are efforts to fashion the character of an organisation both in the way it portrays itself in society and in the promotion of a spirit among employees. It is important to note that such a focus on the character of an organisation is not for any particular moral objective, but it is, in the end, about "spin". It is about how an organisation can present itself for its own particular interests. In fact, organisations often alter their public face as they perceive the public change its attitudes. A clear example of this is the effort of companies to appear "green" because they perceive that the public favours environmental responsibility.

This reveals a truth – character is considered important in the corporate world. It is something celebrated in nations and cultures. And it is something of particular importance for each human being. It is at the personal level that we will investigate the creation of character.

Character – the preoccupation of the ancient philosophers

The nature of character preoccupied the philosophical investigations of the ancient Greeks like Socrates, Plato, Aristotle, and the Stoics. The concept of character was an early area of reflection by the philosophers. When they considered character they saw it as involving the moral dimension of human life. The question of character was not just about certain qualities promoted for their own sake, but rather the formation of the character as the goal of human life. According to these ancient thinkers in Greece who laid the foundations for Western thought, human life concerned the development of the qualities of the person. The wise man was the one who had identified the most noble of human virtues and set out to embody them.

Many of Plato's dialogues explore the nature of virtue and what makes a virtuous person.[1] In these dialogues Plato speaks of Socrates asking questions about what constitutes virtue. The response is couched in behavioral terms. For instance when Laches replies to Socrates' question about what constitutes courage he proposes that courage consists of standing one's ground in battle. Socrates challenges this response by arguing that at times such an action would be foolhardy if the person becomes exposed to needless risk. Plato recognizes that virtue is not found in behaviour but in the interior dispositions of character. It requires a person to have developed a good moral character to be able to determine what actions constitute a true response to a particular situation.

Thus, it is not possible to define rules that determine what constitutes virtue but it is the focus on the quality of character which is able to make sound and appropriate judgements in individual situations.

The Greek philosophers saw that the goal of human life was to live well (*eu zên*) and the fruit of this was happiness (*eudaimonia*). To achieve this state of being, an individual will recognise that there are subordinate goals that need to be placed within the overall goal. The Stoics saw happiness as "living coherently" (*homologoumenôs zên*). Aristotle saw the achievement of a complete (*teleios*) life as achieving full human potential. Arriving at this point means that one's life is worthy of imitation and admiration because it is evident that it has reached a state of human achievement at the personal level. This achievement is not the result of good fortune or learning but is the fruit of virtue. In other words, it is virtuous activity that completes or perfects human life.

In their consideration of the nature of human character, the Greeks recognised that human reality was more than just something understood

---

1 See the so-called "Socratic" dialogues.

in terms of what can be seen, felt and touched. They understood that human existence had a moral dimension. This moral aspect could only be grasped when one understood that the human person had a spiritual dimension to their nature. They proposed the existence of the human soul. They realised that human life cannot be understood in material terms alone. Indeed they understood that it is the spiritual aspect that is the true foundation of the human person and the ultimate source of human growth.

The early philosophers understood that the quality of the human person was fashioned at the spiritual level. They viewed human life as a striving for a quality of human character animated by a moral sense. Socrates, who left no written works, is quoted by Plato as saying:

> To feel confident about the fate of his soul is the right of every man who during life has turned his back upon the pleasures and adornments of the body, looking upon them as alien to him and more likely to do him harm than good; who has been anxious to enjoy the delights of learning: and who, after adorning his soul with no alien trinkets but with the true ornaments of self-restraint, justice, courage, freedom and truth awaits his departure to the other world, ready to march whenever fate may call.[2]

The examination of the nature of the human person led the early philosophers to understand that human life concerns the development of a character adorned by key moral virtues. The true realisation of human life is to be found at the level of the quality of character. The two basic elements in developing character they taught was firstly the appreciation that we have a spiritual dimension to ourselves; that is, we have a soul. Secondly, they realised that character will be fashioned by identifying and pursuing certain moral virtues.

In his book, *Republic*, Plato divides the human soul into three parts: rational, appetitive and spiritual.[3] The rational was seen as the highest

---

2 *Phaedo*, 114c-115a.
3 *Republic,* Book IV.

quality. The appetitive part is base desire. The spiritual he understood as being the pursuit of honour. To be virtuous he proposed we must both understand what contributes to our overall good and have our spiritual and appetitive desires educated properly so that they agree with the guidance provided by the rational part of the soul.

Aristotle, on the other hand, divided the soul into two basic parts: the rational and the non-rational. Of all the Greek moralists, Aristotle provides the most psychologically insightful account of virtuous character. He defines virtuous character in his *Nicomachean Ethics* in these terms:

> Excellence [of character], then, is a state concerned with choice, lying in a mean relative to us, this being determined by reason and in the way in which the man of practical wisdom would determine it.[4]

For Aristotle character is a state of being. It is not feeling nor capacity nor tendency to behave in certain ways but it is a settled condition of who we are. Character means that the non-rational part of ourselves is in union with the rational part of ourselves. Thus, a person of sound character is not wracked by self-doubt. The person is a unified whole and from this unity comes an inner harmony. Virtue requires a harmony between cognitive and affective elements of the person. Virtue is the state that makes a human being good and makes him perform his function well. This for Aristotle is the path to doing good and being happy.

The Greek philosophers explored the subject of character and laid the foundation for a philosophical exploration of the place of virtue in human life. Their particular contribution was to identify the importance of character for true human life. Christian thought would embrace this teaching and raise it to a new level inspired by the revelation of the nature of God and the nature of the human person offered in Jesus of Nazareth, Word of God and Son of Man.

---

4 *Nicomachean Ethics* II.7.

The Christian perspective

For the Christian, human reason is enlightened by faith. Faith exposes the mind to the revelation of truth emanating from God. God is the origin of the human person. God is the Creator who has designed the nature of the human person and has placed his imprint on humanity. Our understanding of ourselves is enhanced when we seek to penetrate the intentions and purposes of God the Creator. To truly understand ourselves we need firstly to consider the intentions of God. In the midst of all of creation human beings are unique. Human beings are the apex of all created reality.

Pope Benedict XVI has often commented on the need to engage both faith and reason in the effort to discover the true nature of human life. He explored this theme in his now famous Regensburg Address. In this address he spoke of the relationship between faith and reason, and considered the place of the interaction between Greek philosophy and Christian faith in fashioning the intellectual and moral culture of Europe, and hence of Western civilisation. He was aware that this rich heritage is currently under very real threat. He proposes that we need to preserve this heritage, and the path forward is the application of both faith and reason working in concert with one another. In this very important paper the Pope sought to lay a foundation for the understanding that the true flourishing of individuals and culture lies in the interaction between faith and reason.

He commented:

> This inner rapprochement between Biblical faith and Greek philosophical inquiry was an event of decisive importance not only from the standpoint of the history of religions, but also from that of world history – it is an event which concerns us even today. Given this convergence, it is not surprising that Christianity, despite its origins and some significant developments in the East, finally took on its historically decisive character in Europe. We can also express this the other way

around: this convergence, with the subsequent addition of the Roman heritage, created Europe and remains the foundation of what can rightly be called Europe.[5]

Faith – Christian faith – and reason, emerging from Greek philosophical thought, converged and became the foundation to a civilization which has enriched the world.

In our quest for an understanding of the human person we will employ both faith and reason. When the human spirit is enlightened by God, and the human mind genuinely seeks the truth, we have a path for building the understanding of how human life can be fashioned. This in turn reveals how human civilisation can flourish. The human mind searches out the meaning of human life. The Christian brings to this search a personal faith and the revelation offered through that faith.

Know Thyself

How well do we really know ourselves? This is an important question today. Modern life can be lived on the surface. Moments of quiet reflection are often drowned out by the constant noise of the society around us. In the age of the "sound bite" many do not take time to reflect on the deeper issues in life. Living can become simply the hasty response to the circumstance of life. There is little reference to sources of wisdom and traditions of thought that are available to us through the history of our civilisation. This is the great temptation today: to ignore or overlook the past. Modernity tends to consider itself sufficient unto itself. There is a desire to be free of any restrictive rules or practices that may be imposed from traditions of the past. Some of us resist the former ways of doing things or prefer to be allowed to find the way for ourselves. This is part of the spirit of our age. Each of us has his or her own history of the experience of life.

---

5 Address by Pope Benedict XVI to the University of Regensburg, 12 September 2006.

Experience is an important teacher. But experience alone is not enough. This is particularly true when our experiences are not subject to reflection and examination. If our age is such that many race from experience to experience and form their impressions and responses on the run, then are we becoming a people lost in superficiality?

The phrase, "know thyself", is carved in stone at Delphi in Greece. This simple statement occupied the thought of Socrates.[6] The Greek philosophers came to the realisation that self-knowledge is the path to virtue and hence happiness. Indeed the ancient Greeks considered that knowledge of oneself opened the door to an insight into all things – the world, the cosmos and divine truth.

The Christian tradition grounded in the Scriptures and developed by the Fathers and Saints pursued this same path. The great Cappadocian Fathers[7] – Saints Basil the Great, Gregory of Nazianzus and Gregory of Nyssa – all of whom were grounded in Greek thought, taught that self knowledge was the basis to sound spiritual and hence personal growth.

Saint Gregory Nazianzus in one of his poems said:

> You have a job to do, soul, and a great one, if you like: examine yourself, what it is you are and how you act, where you come from, and where you are going to end, and whether to live is this very life you are living, or something else besides. You have a job to do, soul: by these things cleanse yourself.[8]

St Basil preached a homily entitled "Give heed to yourself" based on the text of Deuteronomy 15:6. In it he said, "Scrupulous attention to yourself will be of itself sufficient to guide you to the knowledge

---

6 See Zenephon, *Memorabilia*, 4.21. The Ancient Greek aphorism "Know yourself" (Greek: γνῶθι σεαυτόν or *gnothi seauton*) was inscribed in the forecourt of the Temple of Apollo at Delphi.

7 Cappadocia is in modern Turkey. These three great Fathers of the Church lived in the Fourth Century.

8 Poem 2.1.78 *To His Own Soul*

of God. If you give heed to yourself, you will not need to look for signs of the Creator in the structure of the universe; but in yourself, as in a miniature replica of cosmic order, you will contemplate the great wisdom of the Creator." [9]

Clearly the ancients were aware that coming to self-knowledge is a basis upon which one can discover the truth, not only about self but about the reality of things. The pursuit of such knowledge is not a simple matter. We have a capacity for self deception and are tempted to rationalise uncomfortable facts. A seeking of knowledge of oneself must be a rigorous and honest process.

The Contribution of Christian Teaching

In his 2009 address to the new Australian Ambassador to the Holy See, Mr Tim Fischer, the Holy Father said,

> The Church's engagement with civil society is anchored in her conviction that human progress – whether as individuals or communities – is dependent upon the recognition of the supernatural vocation proper to every person. It is from God that men and women receive their essential dignity (cf. Gen 1:27) and the capacity to seek truth and goodness. Within this broad perspective we can counter tendencies to pragmatism and consequentialism, so prevalent today, which engage only with the symptoms and effects of conflicts, social fragmentation, and moral ambiguity, rather than their roots. When humanity's spiritual dimension is brought to light, individuals' hearts and minds are drawn to God and to the marvels of human life: being itself, truth, beauty, moral values, and other persons. In this way a sure foundation to unite society and sustain a vision of hope can be found.[10]

---

9 *Homilia* 3, PG 31:197-98.
10 Reported in *Zenit*, 12 February 2009.

These words of Pope Benedict XVI simply and clearly capture the contribution that Christian faith makes not only to individual life, but to the quality of life in the society.

Formation of Character

This book is about investigating the way in which the Christian tradition has seen the path to the formation of true human character. Such development of character is the way to full human flourishing and a means of finding enduring happiness.

Our investigations must begin with a consideration of the way in which Christians understand the nature of the human person, what we call a Christian anthropology. From this foundation we can then consider the qualities of a truly Christian character, such character will be fully human for it is the discovery of the truth of humanity as intended by God the Creator. We will conclude with a consideration of the path to union with God – holiness of life.

Part 1

Christian Anthropology

1.
Made in the Image of God

Any discussion about character must be based on a clear understanding of the nature of human beings. Thus we must begin our enquiry with a consideration of how we human beings tick. Such a consideration will involve – as we have mentioned – the application both of reason and also the insight we receive through our Christian faith. In other words a Christian anthropology will be a philosophical anthropology. It will incorporate disciplines such as psychology. At the same time it will include theological anthropology drawing on the teaching of the Scripture and the living tradition of the Church, especially that offered by the teaching of the saints who were examples of living the Christian life. The teaching of the saints will be particularly important, as their teaching embodies not only theoretical understanding but the direct experience.

The biblical account of creation describes human beings as created in "the image and likeness of God".[11] What is this "image and likeness"? Immediately it suggests that, as in contrast to the rest of creation, human beings have an element of the divine nature in them. Human beings are an image of God in some way or other. They reflect something, at least, of the nature of God. This gives us our distinctiveness in relation to the rest of creation, and our dignity as human beings.

One immediately evident approach to this question is to view the image of God in human beings as being the existence of the soul. After

---

11 See *Genesis* 1:27. See also *Wisdom* 7:24-28; *Romans* 8:29; 2 *Corinthians* 4:4; *Colossians* 1:15; *Hebrews* 1:3; 1 *John* 3:2.

all, God is spirit and so the character of God in us must be our spiritual aspect, our soul. While this is true we must be careful to avoid the view that the body is somehow of secondary importance, belonging merely to the earth while the soul is that which has final value. This attitude existed in the ancient world, for instance, in Manicheaism[12]. The risk in this approach to the question is that it devalues the human body. Christian faith has always upheld the essential worth of the human body. Christian belief in the Incarnation – "the Word became flesh"! (*John* 1:14) – underpins an understanding that the physical body has its own worth.

In considering this question of image of God in human beings we need to bear in mind that Christ, the Incarnate Son of God, embraced human nature in its totality, except sin. In Christian teaching, Christ, born a man, is the Logos, the Word, the perfect image of God. In his humanity he reveals God to us. The ancient Fathers of the Church in considering this saw Christ to be what God intended human beings to be. Christ was the model according to which God created Adam. Thus we could say that each human being is "an image of the image".

How do we understand this image of God in us? Is it simply that we are persons – on another plane to the animals? God has revealed himself to us as "three persons in one nature". We come to know God as person – God the Father; the Son revealed as the man Jesus; the Holy Spirit as the personification of that love. Thus, the human person, in becoming fully what he or she can be, reflects the image of God. The human person in witnessing to qualities that we identify as those of God Himself – like love, compassion and mercy – reflects the nature of God. The person is becoming as God is.

Made in the image of God, only human beings are capable of

---

[12] Manichaeism is founded on the teaching of the Persian Mani (third century) who claimed that before the existence of heaven and earth there were two Principles, the one Good the other Bad. These two Principles are in constant struggle with each other.

seeking union with God. Human beings alone are able to know and love God. In the well known line of St Augustine this is captured so poignantly: "You have made us for yourself, O Lord, and we are restless until we rest in You".[13] Destined for relationship with God and intended for union with God, human beings are the only aspect of creation willed by God for its own sake.[14] Human beings then have a unique dignity.

Furthermore, each human being possesses as essential to his or her being, self-knowledge, self-possession and the capacity of entering into relationships with other persons. Such relationships are grounded in love and self-giving. This reflects another aspect to the uniqueness of human beings made in the "image and likeness of God". God Himself is perfect self-knowledge and self-possession and "God is love" (*1 John* 4:8). Our capacity to form relationships with other human beings as well as with God Himself is testimony to our sharing in the nature of God. This is the dignity that is ours as human beings.

Composition of the Human Person

As we have noted, Greek philosophy recognised that each person is composed of a material component and a spiritual component – commonly called body and soul. The Scriptures describe the human being as being created from the dust of the earth, and then the Book of Genesis says that the Creator "blew the breath of life into his nostrils and man became a living being" (*Genesis* 2:7).

The existence of the soul may not be self-evident to people these days. Many have adopted a materialist view of the human person. Many are more comfortable with seeing themselves as the result of an evolutionary process over the eons. Human beings, they believe, are just more advanced in a continuum with the rest of nature. The distinctiveness of human beings is simply that they have evolved more.

---

13 *Confessions*, Lib 1,1-2,2.5,5.
14 See *Catechism of the Catholic Church*, n. 356.

The idea of a soul is foreign to this scientific view of the nature of humanity. Yet, while people will comfortably see themselves this way, they do experience a yearning for transcendence. There are moments when people grapple with a sense that there is something more. Often when confronted with death, either in someone close to themselves or when their own mortality is experienced through disease or a life threatening encounter, many people find themselves seeking something beyond.

It is also a curious fact that as many have been led to a purely scientific understanding of life and have discarded the traditional Christian understanding, there has been a proliferation of "New Age" ideas that result in normally rational people embracing all sorts of exotic concepts concerning a transcendent world.

The soul should not be seen as a separate part of the human person but rather understood as the spiritual aspect of each individual. The soul informs the body. The soul is the spiritual principle, our most inner self, and the distinguishing feature of being a human being.

The question of the relationship of body and soul is an intriguing one. For a human being the soul and body are a unity making up the person. We are not composed of two natures – one bodily and one spiritual – rather we are a union of body and soul that makes one nature, the human person. We can speak of the two dimensions of ourselves: we are at one time living both an outer and an inner life.

The outer life is what prominently dominates our daily existence, yet it is the perishable part of ourselves. Each day we are one day closer to death. Our inner life is the more mysterious, and yet the more vital, in terms of our daily living. This inner life is the life of our thoughts, our emotions, our decisions, our interaction with the world about us. It is this inner life that is open to the divine, and is intended for union with the divine. When we consider the nature of our life we see that the inner life, the life of the soul, is the animating element to our being.

A further question is raised here in relation to a Christian anthropology. Having agreed that each person is composed of a body and soul, Christian revelation, particularly in the New Testament, speaks of a tripartite division of body-soul-spirit. In his *Letter to the Thessalonians*, St Paul says, "May your spirit, life and body be kept blameless for the coming of our Lord Jesus Christ" (*1 Thessalonians* 5:23) and in the *Letter to the Hebrews* the word of God is described as "something alive and active: it cuts more incisively than any two-edged sword: it can seek out the place where soul is divided from spirit" (*Hebrews* 4:12).

The human person is a composite of body and soul. We are conscious of this reality at a psychological level. We could say that our soul gives life to our body. Who we are as bodily persons is animated by our human soul, the seat of our individuality. Christian faith teaches us and the tradition of the Church witnesses to the presence of the indwelling Spirit of God. It is this Spirit that brings to birth our spiritual life, our life in God who is spirit. Just as the body, made from the dust of the earth is animated by the soul, so the soul is animated by the Holy Spirit and brings it to life.

The Life of the Soul

Let us explore further the life of the soul. The early Christian writer, Origen, raised questions that occupied the first Christian thinkers: "Is the soul corporeal or incorporeal, simple or composite? Is it, as some believe, contained in the semen of the body, or does it come in a complete state from outside to clothe the already formed body?"[15] Can we experience the presence of the soul within us? Can we feel the soul? And how is the soul transmitted to us? Is it transmitted – as Origen asks – from parent to child?

Catholic teaching on this question was hammered out in the Middle Ages by theologians like St Thomas Aquinas. Basing himself

---

15 *In Canticum* 1.2 PG 13:126-127.

in Aristotelian philosophy he taught that the soul, though the form of the body, is simple and is capable of acting independently of the body. The Church has addressed the question of the transmission of the soul to each individual and teaches that "every spiritual soul is created immediately by God"[16] and it is not therefore transmitted by parents to offspring. The soul is not inherited but, as a unique creation of God, has a unique relationship with God and, thus, the human person is capable of coming into a unique personal relationship with God.

Yet the soul is intimately engaged with the life of the body. The human soul – or the carnal *pneuma* as it is sometimes described – can follow the body in earthly pursuits, or, spurred on by the Spirit, can rise in its own spiritual pursuits. In his poem, *De anima* (Concerning the Soul) St Gregory Nazianzus wrote, "The soul is the breath of God and it submits to the mixture with the earthly element even though it is of heavenly origin. It is a light hidden in a cave, but nonetheless divine and imperishable."[17]

The soul then is not constrained by the body, and has the capacity of raising the person to moral and spiritual heights. This understanding follows both the revelation provided by Christian faith and accords with the investigations of the ancient philosophers. Faith and reason are in harmony on this question.

The notions of Mind and Heart

While exploring the nature of the human soul we need to investigate other ways of considering the nature of the inner life of the human person. Two commonly used notions attempting to situate the essence of the life of the soul are those of "mind" and "heart".

For the Greeks the mind – *nous* – was the highest human faculty, and the focus of the life of the soul. Plato saw the pure exercise of

---

16 *Catechism of the Catholic Church*, n. 366.
17 *Caminum liber* 1.1.8 vv 1-3. PG 37:446.

reason as "that which is best in the soul".[18] Those Fathers of the Church influenced by Greek thought, especially Platonism, would follow this line and thus would see the mind as the point of the soul's interaction with God. Thus, prayer would be described as a raising of the mind to God.[19]

But the notion of heart has won over in Christian thought and experience. Here the Christian mystic has contributed significantly. Would we today view the mind as the centre and focus of our being? Contemporary consideration of this question would more likely lean towards the concept of the heart. The biblical world, certainly, would be on our side, and would view the heart as the centre of the human person and the point of contact with the divine. The cry of David in the Miserere, *Psalm 51*, reflects the biblical anthropology: "God, create in me a clean heart" (*Psalm* 51:10).

What do we mean by the heart? It is an ambiguous concept. It is best seen as a psychological term rather than a philosophical term. The notion of the heart as being the core of the person makes it more than the seat of our affective life. This is a common way in which the word is used: "I love you with all my heart". The biblical notion will see the term in a much wider meaning. The heart incorporates all our inner powers. It is the state of our heart that reveals the true nature of ourselves. We may put on an outward show, but in our hearts lies the truth of ourselves. The Prophet Samuel was told that while man looks at appearances, God looks at the heart (*1 Samuel* 16:17). We know this. We can reveal what we would want to show to the world, but

---

18 *Phaedrus* 247c.

19 An example of this is the thought of Evagrius Ponticus. Evagrius was a Christian Platonist. Following Greek philosophy he emphasises the role of the mind. For Evagrius the goal of the Christian life is the human soul, purified from all worldly ambitions, capable of contemplating God in his essence. So he wrote in his *Chapters on Prayer*, "Prayer is a continuous intercourse of the mind with God" (Ch. 3) and "Prayer is the ascent of the mind to God" (Ch. 35). For Evagrius the mind is the highest human faculty.

inwardly we can be quite different. Thus, for instance, we say, "I will put on a brave face". To outsiders it would appear that I am confident and sure of myself while, in fact, I am frightened and confused. What is in my heart is the real state of my being.

In common speech we tend towards referring to the heart as that which is the core of ourselves. The heart is the principle of human integration. All the forces of body and soul are drawn together in the heart. The heart is my "I". It is in the end the principle of my inner unity. It is what makes sense of the multitude of my actions and their motivation.

The heart, too, is the battlefield between the forces of good and evil. Thus, Christ teaches that the greatest commandment is to love God "with all your heart", and your neighbour as yourself (*Matthew* 22:37; 39). Indeed, evil can take root in the heart and comes forth in actions that defile the person, as the Lord teaches.[20] The teaching of Jesus contains many references to the heart. The notion of heart is a key focus of his effort to move people from viewing things at the exterior level alone. God is interested in the state of the heart and not just in the outward observance of laws and customs.

The Christian spiritual tradition highlights the importance of the heart. Writing under the name of St Macarius, a fourth century Syrian monk wrote fifty homilies that present a spirituality of the heart. Thus he says, "The heart directs and governs all the other organs of the body".[21]

With the notion of heart goes that of feelings. Here, in the thought of Christian writers, feelings are more than affective states but rather refer to the movements within the person combining the mind, the will and the emotions. Feelings incline us to respond to something imagined as good or evil. They are the link between the senses and the

---

20 See *Matthew* 15:19ff.
21 St Macarius, *Homily*, 15, 20.

mind. The most important feeling is love and this is what inclines us towards a perceived good.[22] Feelings receive a great deal of attention these days. People speak about doing what they "feel is right". There is confusion here between a certain emotion and what in fact may be coming from another source, their conscience (the next subject to be considered).

We need to make another comment about feelings. Our emotions are often appealed to in advertising and in the media generally. A person who acts merely in response to feelings is an immature person. Our human actions need to engage not only feelings, but also our intellect. Indeed the notion of the heart can be understood at that place in ourselves where reasoning and emotion meet and combine to guide our actions.

The seat of the moral life

For the ancients, the soul was the seat of our moral life. Seneca speaks of a spirit abiding within us as "one who marks our good and bad deeds."[23] The Greeks spoke of a faculty – they named it *syneidesis* – which evoked a sense of moral wellbeing or sense of guilt. The Fathers of the Church spoke of a special faculty implanted in us by God that shows the mind what is good and what is bad.[24] We call this faculty *conscience*.

When we consider our experience of the workings of our conscience, we notice that it is not only a judgement after the fact – producing wellbeing or guilt – but it is an active agent bearing on the mind inducing us to recognise the moral significance of a concrete act which we are about to perform. We know it as a "voice" within – often quiet yet persistent – which encourages us towards that which is good

---

[22] See *Catechism of the Catholic Church* on the passions, nn. 1764-1766.
[23] *Epistle* 41.1
[24] Dorotheos, *Instructions* 3.20.

and meritorious, and warning us of that which is morally suspect.

Conscience is a faculty that every person possesses, yet the degree of its influence on our actions does depend on how much we are attuned to its voice. St Augustine stated wisely, "Return to your conscience, question it … Turn inward brethren, and in everything you do, see God as your witness".[25] Conscience can be dulled by excessive wrongdoing and limited in its capacity to guide us aright by lack of sound formation. Conscience, then, is not an infallible agent and actually requires careful nurturing so that it is able to assist us for the best results.

A conscience appreciated and heeded provides each human being with the capacity to recognise and pursue those things that are right and best for human life. In conscience a person finds a source for his or her true dignity as a responsible and wise human being.

At the present time there is much focus on conscience as the justification for moral choices. In an age that emphasises the individual and the right to self determination, conscience is often invoked as a source of justification for doing what a person considers to be right. Conscience then becomes a tool for self-will. This approach, which can be called a "cafeteria" approach to morality, results in people selecting those moral positions that fit with their own views and leave those that do not accord with their perceptions. One hears them comment that they are following their conscience. In fact it has become the justification for moral relativism, which is endemic in contemporary Western culture. Invoking conscience is seen as giving justification for decisions that are not grounded in either reference to authoritative guides or in serious rational consideration of the moral issue. Personal feelings, which are often simply perceptions and views that have been formed from all sorts of idiosyncratic sources, are the guide to moral choices. The Frank Sinatra mantra, "I did it my way," expresses the spirit of the time. The brand *Nike* urges us to "just do it".

---

25 In *Ep Jo.* 8.9. PL 35.2041.

Clearly there is a need to rediscover the true nature of conscience. Here, again, we can turn to the wisdom of the ancient philosophers and to consistent Christian teaching.

Freedom

The existence of conscience reminds us of our capacity to make moral decisions. We have a capacity to choose what is right and good, or to decide to take paths that are wrong and even evil. Each human being has a fundamental freedom to make moral decisions and to choose paths of behaviour that will shape the nature of their character. Christians reflecting on the creative act of God realised that individual freedom was at the heart of human nature. Against the Stoics who proposed fatalism, the Fathers, like Justin Martyr, saw that freedom was the basis for merit. St Irenaeus expressed the issue frankly when he said, "Man is rational and therefore like God; he is created with freewill and is master over his acts".[26] As human beings then, the exercise of our freedom takes precedence over everything else. In our freedom is to be found our dignity – the dignity that has been given to us by the Creator.

Influenced by the preoccupation of the Greek philosophers in the attainment of knowledge, the Fathers came to see the inherent link between freedom and knowledge. The pursuit of knowledge – truth – is the means to virtue. In choosing to seek truth we exercise our freedom and provide the platform for the ennobling of our life. We recognise the truth and, using our freedom, embrace it. The dictum of Christ best expresses this: "you will come to know the truth, and the truth will set you free" (*John* 8:32).

Is freedom found in the soul in its human or in its spiritual dimension? Certainly the will is a faculty of the human soul. The will is the instrument for the exercise of our freedom. The traditions of the Christian East, especially that sponsored by the monks in the desert,

---

26 *Adv Haeres* 4.4.3. PG 7.1.983.

postulated that freedom was an element of the spiritual dimension of the soul. The monks saw the attainment of *apatheia* – passionlessness[27] – as the goal of the inner moral and spiritual struggle. Apatheia suggests a state of being whereby one is "above" earthly passions, and so free.

Attitude to the Body

The ancient Christian attitude towards the body is a controversial issue for today's mentality. Our age glories in the human body and it is the subject of endless consideration. The amount of literature and attention given to the enhancement of the body suggests a fixation – diets, fashion, exercise, cosmetic surgery. Our society tends to have a narcissistic preoccupation with body image, while the ancients appear to view the body as the "tomb of the soul".[28] Plato considered that the soul's task was to be freed from the "fetters of the flesh".[29] The body was viewed as the enemy of the soul. It was seen by the Stoics as useful at best. Epicletis stated, "In things pertaining to the body, do not go further than mere usefulness".[30]

This attitude influenced a number of the Fathers of the Church and gave rise not only to a pessimistic view of the body, but allowed this idea to carry over into a consideration of human sexuality.

Christianity has been accused of being anti-body and anti-sex. This accusation is not without grounds. Yet it does not do justice to the biblical picture, the true source for Christian understanding. The story of Genesis clearly expresses that all that God created was good: "God saw all he had made, and indeed it was very good" (*Genesis* 1:31). The Christian mystery clearly testifies to the ultimate dignity of the body in

---

27 This is an inadequate meaning to a term revered by the monks. The term reflects that state of being whereby the mind is free from earthly passions (pathos). It is a state of victory over carnal desires.

28 See Plato, *Gorgias* 493a.

29 See *Phaedo* 67d.

30 *The Encheiridion* 33.7

its doctrine of the Resurrection of the Body. The human body while on earth is subject to struggle, and suffering is destined to be transformed into a glorious body freed from all imperfections.

The Scriptures use two different words to describe the body – *soma* and *sarx*, in Greek, translated usually as "body" and "flesh". The "body" is that created by God and it is good. The "flesh" is our carnal nature that seeks satisfaction for its needs. It is the place of the basic appetites and passions. The flesh is burdened by sin and its tendency is to drag us down. This is that part of us that needs to be disciplined and overcome.

Distinguishing these two aspects to our bodily nature enables us to see the truth in the teaching of the ancients, while at the same time gives us a healthy approach to our bodily existence.

The two modalities of the human person: Male and Female

Human beings exist in two modalities: they are either male or female. This is evident in their bodily nature, but it is not limited to physical characteristics. Human beings experience themselves as being masculine or feminine.

The question of the understanding of what constitutes masculinity and femininity is much debated today. The feminist movement emerging with particular vigour in the last decades of the previous century[31] focused on equality of rights and dignity for women. While there is much to commend in this movement it did obscure some aspects of the nature of femininity (and hence masculinity). There was an orientation to seeing women as being the same as men. What was lost was a clear sense of the complementary nature of men and women. The pursuit of equality does not have to suppress the true character of femininity.

---

31 There was an earlier feminist movement at the beginning of twentieth century. This movement was involved particularly with the right to vote.

The challenge today is to appreciate the true nature of sexual identity. In other words, what it means to be a woman and a man. Sexual identity belongs not just to the body, but to the person. Equality and dignity does not require surrender of sexual identity, but can be found through sexual identity. Self fulfilment is not denied if one seeks to be fully man or woman. Indeed the human person, being realised in two modalities needs the full expression of each to ensure that humanity is properly realised. Society is incomplete if masculinity or femininity are not appropriately realised respectively in each person.

The key to this is the complementary nature of man and woman. Human nature is realised in two expressions which are meant to complete each other, and not to be in some sort of competition with each other. Indeed, men need women to be fully women (that is, embracing their femininity to the full) in order to complement their masculinity, and vice versa. Society is built on the ways in which men and women contribute to each other from their masculinity or femininity.

The complementary nature of man and woman has one vital purpose – it is designed to provide the ground for a man and a woman to enter the lifelong exclusive union of marriage. In the account of creation given in the Book of Genesis, the description of the creation of woman from the rib of man is immediately followed by these words, "and that is why a man leaves his father and mother and joins himself to his wife and the two become one"[32]. One particular injunction is given to human beings – having entered such unions – "'Be fruitful, multiply, fill the earth" (*Genesis* 1:28). The plan of God for human life is that man and woman would embrace a married existence which would provide the stable environment of love and security into which children could be born and nurtured. Marriage has two purposes – a lifelong union of complementary companionship grounded in mutual

---

32 See the second creation account *Genesis* 2: 22-24.

love and respect, and the generation of new life which is nurtured by the contribution of both a father and a mother.

The argument being proposed today of the right for people who have a same sex attraction to be able to enter marriage is based on a false premise. It is self evident that marriage is the complementary union of a man and woman. This is how we are designed. This is the plan and purpose of the Creator. A union of people of the same sex, by definition, cannot be a marriage. It is simply against what is intended by nature.

2.
The Question of Good and Evil

Our appreciation of nature around us leads us to marvel at the beauty and the intricacy of the material universe. It is a wonder. It stirs the human spirit whether it is looking into the cosmos or watching a sunset or observing a simple insect. The Scriptures declare unequivocally that all God created was good: "God saw all that he had made and indeed it was very good" (*Genesis* 1:31). The divine arrangement of created reality readily witnesses to beauty and is testimony to the providential wisdom of God. Yet the waters that give life can become powerfully destructive in flood or storm. Nature is a resource for human life but can also inflict great suffering. Human beings made in the image of God can witness to heroic self-giving or become callously cruel. In human beings we see the face of evil as well as good. Where does evil originate?

This will now be our enquiry. It is a baffling question for humanity. The problem of evil is a stumbling block for many in their efforts to come to faith in a loving God. The existence of evil challenges people and they quite reasonably ask: How can a loving God allow such suffering?

The biblical account of the creation of human beings recounts that the human person was given the gift of personal freedom. God placed before human beings the opportunity of moral choice – the biblical text speaks of the tree of good and evil.[33] In this story choosing

---
[33] See *Genesis* 2:17, "Nevertheless of the tree of the knowledge of good and evil you are not to eat, for on the day you shall eat of it you shall most surely die".

good is the way to choose life. Choosing evil is the way of choosing death. The story of the fall of Adam and Eve, told in *Genesis*, chapter 3, is the story of every human being. Each of us has the freedom to choose either good or evil. When evil is chosen evil is released in the world. We become the authors of our own destruction. We abandon the Garden of Eden and discover life as a struggle and subject to pain.

This is the testimony of Scripture and the teaching of the Church. Human beings used their God-given freedom to choose against God. There was a moment of the original act of choice of evil rather than good: the original sin that fundamentally changed the relationship between God and humanity, and the harmony of human beings with creation. The Christian, though, can never view this without reference to the intention of God to redress the situation by an act of redemption to be realised in sending his Son.

What Christian faith teaches about evil is that firstly there is no eternal principle of evil. Good and Evil are not equal and opposites. God acquiesces (using the term of St John Chrysostom[34]), allowing evil to take place. God does not create or cause evil, but permits it. The existence of evil is the price that we have to pay for our freedom. We human beings have introduced evil into the world.

God can enable evil to be turned to good. The *Exsultet* hymn sung at the Easter Vigil in the Catholic liturgy says, "O happy fault, O necessary sin of Adam, that gained for us so great a Redeemer!" God permitted sin but more wonderfully restored humanity by sending his Son as saviour.

The effect of evil on humanity

What is the effect of the advent of evil upon human beings? Are we permanently and fundamentally corrupted? There is no doubt about the flawed nature of human beings. Our experience is that we are all born afflicted by a tendency to do evil. Catholic theology speaks of

---

[34] See *On the Statutes* 65.5 PG 49:88a.

the presence of Original Sin in each person.[35] Our human nature is not permanently corrupted, however, but rather wounded. We are subject to suffering and death. Each person experiences an inclination to evil – theology calls it "concupiscence".[36] We know this experience well. We find ourselves moved to frustration or laziness or deception. We can't explain where it comes from, but it is there. It is real.

The existence of evil, the mystery of pain and suffering, the spectre of death, puzzle human thought. The Christian understanding is that it can be traced to an Original Sin. This primordial act of freedom was an act of deciding for self rather than God, or, putting it another way, choosing disobedience rather than obedience. Coming to recognise this truth has far-reaching implications for how we view our life in the world.

Accepting this interpretation of the human condition is vitally important in our approach to education, morality and politics. In fact our understanding of the origin and working of evil will largely determine how we address the issue of the formation of character. It may be tempting to want to pretend that I am master of myself, and that I do not need to be accountable for what stirs within me. We sometimes hear people say that everyone else has to accept them as they are (when they do something wrong). This is an extreme individualism which seeks to avoid any accountability for one's actions. Such a person is admitting that they cannot manage themselves.

Societies can bypass the notion of moral responsibility and seek to ensure social cohesion by the implementation of regulations – like

---

[35] The *Catechism of the Catholic Church* teaches, "Adam and Eve transmitted to their descendants human nature wounded by their own first sin and hence deprived of original holiness and justice; this deprivation is called 'original sin'" (n. 417).

[36] The *Catechism of the Catholic Church* expresses this experience in these words, "As a result of original sin, human nature is weakened in its powers, subject to ignorance, suffering and the domination of death, and inclined to sin (this inclination is called "concupiscence")" (n. 418).

the law to wear a seatbelt. Such societies will also rely on education to shape the attitude of citizens. Governments spend much money on advertising campaigns which promote certain modes of behaviour. And they are not without success – consider the anti-litter campaigns or encouragements to engage in a healthy lifestyle. While such campaigns can achieve results they cannot replace the need for each person to assume responsibility for the quality of their moral life. Advertising campaigns will not overcome the reality of concupiscence. At the present time societies are putting more and more regulation in place to address problems. Excessive regulation and the necessity of accountability of compliance can become a burden for citizens. Society will function best when its citizens are inspired interiorly to live a moral life.

Temptation, Oppression, Possession

Let us consider how we experience evil impacting on our lives. We can identify three "levels": temptation, oppression and possession.

The experience of temptation is a daily reality for all human beings. It begins when the alarm goes off – we struggle to get out of bed. We may experience bad thoughts – of jealousy, anger, frustration. It can be the simple constraints of polite society or threat of legal action against us that prevents us from giving in to such temptations. But we also regularly fail: we say something we later regret, or we react angrily to some provocation. We are constantly having to battle with temptation of one kind or another.

We experience temptation from the false allurements of the world around us. Advertisers urge us to live for ourselves, to satisfy basic cravings for comfort and success. We are shown images of happiness that are essentially hollow. Through media in its extraordinary variety of forms we are constantly being tempted. Indeed, there is such an all pervasive attractiveness to live for ourselves that we can become used to it. What is really selfish or shallow or crude becomes part of the landscape of our daily lives. We become deadened in our sensitivity because such temptations are so much the environment in which we live.

We experience temptation as a voice within us seductively suggesting the ways we can satisfy our basic cravings. We have an awareness of an active agent bent on drawing us into what we realise is wrong, a subtle tempting whispering in our ear. Christian thought speaks of the devil as a personal spiritual being engaged in tempting us along a path of wrong.[37]

Christian experience has taught that we are tempted by "the world, the devil and the flesh" From his *Catechetical Instruction on the Apostles' Creed*, St Thomas Aquinas writes: "We know that every temptation is either from the world or the flesh or the devil".

There is a deeper level of struggle that we have to face. This can be called oppression. This is the case where we experience a very strong drive to do something that we know is damaging to ourselves or to others. It can be smoking, binge drinking, stealing. This is the area of addictions. A person here senses the power of an attraction to do something which is damaging to themselves which they experience as quite overwhelming. There is the feeling that the addiction is too strong to resist. Our freedom to decide is diminished. This attraction is oppressive. We can find that giving in to the craving only makes it more difficult to resist next time. We can find that we have become trapped. This is most apparent in the drug addict or the alcoholic.

The third experience of evil is rare, but real. It is the situation when one is possessed by an evil power. While such occurrences are rare,

---

[37] Catholic teaching affirms a constantly held belief in the existence of the devil, or Satan, as a real personal being, a fallen angel, intent on drawing human beings away from the paths of virtue and goodness. The *Catechism of the Catholic Church* teaches, "Behind the disobedient choice of our first parents lurks a seductive voice, opposed to God, which makes them fall into death out of envy. Scripture and the Church's Tradition see in this being a fallen angel, called "Satan" or the "devil". The Church teaches that Satan was at first a good angel, made by God" (n. 391).

they come about because the person has in some way surrendered their freedom to Evil, either by being duped or by complicity with evil. Such possession witnesses to the fact that evil is not just a moral option, but is an active and personal force. As we saw, Christian experience is aware of the existence of the devil and of evil spirits. This is based on the witness of the Scriptures, especially instanced in the ministry of Jesus Christ.

This is the human reality. Our experience is that daily life is a struggle. Character is forged in this struggle. Each of us is engaged in this interior battle. We experience temptation to do wrong. We experience a moral struggle to rise above more base thoughts and desires. We experience this also as a spiritual battle as we recognise that the moral struggle debases the quality of our spiritual well being.

St Paul graphically expresses this spiritual battle in his Letter to the Ephesians:

> Put on the full armour of God so as to be able to resist the devil's tactics. For it is not against human enemies that we have to struggle, but against the principalities and the ruling forces who are masters of the darkness in this world, the spirits of evil in the heavens. That is why you must take up all God's armour, or you will not be able to put up any resistance on the evil day, or stand your ground even though you exert yourselves to the full.
> (*Ephesians* 6:11-13)

We also meet evil in various manifestations in the world around us. We constantly witness acts of evil and witness the suffering of others due to evil done to or around them. War, famine, political domination are some examples of what is the daily content of the news. Sometimes evil impinges painfully on our lives through acts of injustice, or hatred or violence. We not only see evil done to others, but are victims ourselves.

This is the sad lot of being human. It is the reality of the fallen human condition.

3.
In Need of Redemption

St Paul in his *Letter to the Romans* gives a lengthy consideration of the human experience of sin and comments on his own personal experience: "So I find this rule, that for me, where I want to do nothing but good, evil is close at my side". He acutely senses the presence and attraction of evil. He feels himself its prisoner, though he sorely wants to do good. Finally in an expression of exasperation he cries out: "What a wretched man I am! Who will rescue me from this body doomed to death?" (*Romans* 7:24)

We can identify with his experience as it is so with us. Daily life is burdened with an interior struggle. We want to do good, but we find ourselves susceptible to the tendency to evil. This weighs us down. We can be tempted to succumb as it becomes all too hard. Is this not the lot of humanity?

After crying out in seemingly desperation – "Who can save me from this body doomed to death?" – St Paul then adds: "God – thanks be to him – through Jesus Christ our Lord". This statement needs investigation. It presents the kernel of the Christian notion of salvation. We are saved by an action of God through Jesus Christ.

The self-will of humanity, the choice of evil, ruptured the harmony of creation. It also damaged the relationship between God and humanity. Just as any action of rejection in a relationship causes a fracturing of unity, mutual trust and openness in that relationship, so the choice of sin by human beings has fractured the relationship between Creator and creatures.

When a relationship is fractured, one of the parties needs to set on the path of restoring the original unity. Usually it is left to the guilty party to seek reconciliation. The expression of genuine remorse and a humble attitude of seeking forgiveness is the best path.

This is how it is between two equals, but in the case of the situation of humanity's gross rejection of God it is not so easy. It is God, the injured party, who has taken the initiative. The way God has chosen to act is beyond expectation. God the Father would send his Son to effect an act of atonement by offering himself as a sacrificial victim to redeem the relationship between God and humanity. Jesus Christ would offer himself in an act of obedience and become a sacrifice offered on behalf of humanity. He would die on the cross for us.

But first he would embrace the human condition and reveal in his person and his teaching the true nature of God, as a God of mercy and compassion. He would be born in the humblest of conditions, he would seek no position of power or authority, he would move among the poor and suffering, and with words and actions he would reveal the intention of God to save and restore.

Jesus the redeemer of humanity

St Luke the writer of the third Gospel describes Jesus at the commencement of his public ministry going to the synagogue in his own town of Nazareth. He chooses and reads a passage from the prophet Isaiah: "The spirit of the Lord in on me, for he has anointed me to bring good news to the afflicted". Jesus in choosing this passage at the very beginning of his public ministry just after his baptism in the Jordan is wishing to describe his understanding of what his ministry is to be about. The reading continues, "He has sent me to proclaim liberty to captives, sight to the blind, to let the oppressed go free, to proclaim a year of favour from the Lord" (*Luke* 4:18-19).

If this is a "vision statement" that Jesus sees as capturing what his mission is, then we can look at the actions and words of Jesus in this light. Clearly the text proposes that Jesus sees his mission as one of liberation for those captured or oppressed in one way or another. It is not just physical ailments that concern Jesus, but rather the way in which the spirit of humanity is bound and afflicted.

When we turn to St Mark's Gospel we note that the first miracle recorded is that of Jesus in the synagogue being confronted by and then casting out a demon (*Mark* 1:21-28). What is of interest is that the demon initiates the confrontation calling out, "What do you want with us, Jesus of Nazareth? Have you come to destroy us?" It is as though evil is threatened by the presence of Jesus. It suggests that this is the battle that is about to be waged. God through Jesus is going to challenge the free reign that evil has had over the lives of people. The Gospels record a number of instances of such confrontations.

While the mentality of the time readily ascribed to demons forms of oppression that afflicted people, today we might be more circumspect in attributing some afflictions to the influence of demons, explaining such conditions in psychological terms. However, as we have seen already, we cannot eliminate the influence and power of demonic forces. The Church has recognised this. In the celebration of the Sacrament of Baptism there is a prayer of exorcism and other references to the reality of the devil. Through the Church's experience over the centuries the *Rite of Exorcism* has evolved.

As we mentioned previously the human experience of obsessions – like gambling, pornography or substance abuse – reveals a destructive power beyond the capacity of the individual to deal with. Another human experience is that of being assailed by forms of darkness that can simply overwhelm a person – such experiences can be fears of various kinds, memories of rejection or injustice, depression, a sense of worthlessness. These are very real and can be quite debilitating. Some can be addressed by the use of the discipline of psychology and some alleviated by medication. Others may need direct spiritual help to enable them overcome this real debilitating power which is a burden for their lives. Added to these experiences are others that could be termed torments of the soul – for instance an enduring bitterness, an irrational jealousy. These are the "demons" which infest our lives. In our common speech we speak about "facing our demons". Such experiences mean that the person is not free. The person may be substantially burdened and in the grip of forces over which they have little or no control.

There is a graphic story told in some detail by St Mark. It is the story of the Geresene demoniac.[38] The description of the demoniac is a picture of a person being destroyed by powers that consume him. We are told that he lived among the tombs. He would howl and harm himself with stones. It is a picture of a human being robbed of dignity. When we meet such people we are filled with pity: this is not what a human being should be.

In this story Jesus drives out the demons – in this case there are many, "legion" – and the final picture is of a man, calm, clothed and in his right mind. He is a man restored to his proper human dignity.

Jesus declared as he began his public ministry that the "Kingdom of God is close at hand". This declaration proposes that God is acting to bring about a restoration of humanity, to rescue it from the powers of darkness. In one interesting piece of teaching Jesus speaks about himself as coming to take over the house of a "strong man" (*Matthew* 12:29). To do this he will bind the strong man and in a graphic image he posits himself as being in contest with one who has controlled things to date but his time has run out. The stronger one, namely Jesus, has arrived.

The accounts of the many miracles of Jesus, be they physical or spiritual, give testimony to the fact that he has come to bring restoration to humanity suffering under the weight of afflictions of various kinds. Yet his brief three years of public ministry were localised in a particular place and time. What he revealed in those short years was a sign of what he was going to do for all time and for all peoples.

---

38 See *Mark* 5:1-20.

The power of the cross

His mission was intended not just to be a sign of God revealing his concern for humanity, but it was to be a decisive intervention that would change the status quo – the "ancient curse" would be broken and humanity would be redeemed.

Jesus comments that he did not come to be served – as was his due as the Son of God – but to serve and "to give his life as a ransom for many" (*Matthew* 20:28). This final comment of his reveals his understanding that his life was not just encompassed by his good works but he would offer himself as "a ransom for many". In other words, he would pay the price for setting humanity free from the yoke of evil.

The Gospels record the many occasions where Jesus spoke about his forthcoming passion and death. Such predictions were not received well by his disciples who were unable to grasp their meaning and often became frightened by the prospect. St Mark describes the journey to Jerusalem with Jesus walking on ahead, and the disciples "who followed were apprehensive" (*Mark* 10:32).

The suffering and death of Jesus was, at the human level, prompted by the jealousy of the Jewish religious leaders and the compliance of the Roman Governor wishing to avoid social unrest. Yet the Gospels testify that this was all within the intention of God.

The capture of Jesus in the Garden of Gethsemane was absolutely beyond the comprehension of his disciples. Overcome with confusion and fear they all ran away. When Jesus had spoken earlier of his impending passion and death Peter said, "this must not happen to you". Jesus' retort was stinging, "Get behind me Satan! You are an obstacle in my path, because you are thinking not as God thinks but as human beings do" (*Matthew* 16:23). The disciples would only gradually come to grasp why it had to be this way and this would only become clear following his Resurrection.[39]

The purpose of the death of Christ on the cross is the core of the Christian understanding of human life. It is the heart of Christian anthropology. "It was necessary for the Christ to suffer" as the act of redemption of humanity. The writings of the New Testament examine this theme over and over again. St Paul in his *Letter to the Romans* realised that the disobedience of Adam was to be counteracted by the obedience of Christ.[40] In the *Letter to the Philippians*, St Paul captured it beautifully when he wrote that Jesus took on the form of a servant in being born a man and then humbled himself further and became obedient "even to accepting death, death on a cross" (*Philippians* 2:8).

The *Letter to the Hebrews* also explores this theme presenting Jesus as a high priest offering the perfect sacrifice.[41] The notion of sacrifice, commonly understood by the Jews and indeed commonly understood in many ancient religions, highlights an important human realisation that evil must be atoned for. Evil cannot be condoned and once evil has been enacted an act of atonement is required to reverse its damage. Thus the "perfect sacrifice" of Jesus Christ in dying on

---

[39] The account of the two disciples on the way to Emmaus being joined by the Lord and the conversation that ensued captures this theme. The disciples, even hearing of the Resurrection, could not comprehend the significance of what had happened to Jesus. He needed to explain to them why he had to die, "starting from Moses and the Prophets" (*Luke* 24:44-45).

[40] *Romans* 5:19 "For as through the one man's disobedience the many were made sinners, even so through the obedience of the One the many will be made righteous"

[41] The *Letter to the Hebrews* presents a rich theology of Christ as priest. It highlights the significance of the death of Christ where he was both priest and victim. So the Letter speaks of Christ as being able to sympathize with human weakness, since he was tempted/tested as we are, although without sinning himself (4:15). Christ offers sacrifices and prayers only for others, not for himself, since he is sinless and perfect (5:15; 7:2628; 9:14). He offered himself as a sacrifice once for all time (7:27; 9:12, 14, 26; 10:10, 14) and his sacrifice is perfect, since he is perfect/sinless (7:26, 28; 9:14).

the cross accomplished the atonement for the sins of mankind across all time. It was a once-and-for-all action made by the Son of God as a human being, representing humanity before his Father.

The death of Christ on the cross is the way God has chosen to confront the existence of evil. God would, in fact, allow evil to seem to conquer when Christ was being crucified, but in the very act of evil seeming to triumph, God would be victorious. The death of Christ on the cross was the chosen way in which God would overcome the power of evil over humanity once and for all. The victim became the victor. Indeed death itself – the price humanity has paid for its disobedience – was conquered by the fact that death could not contain Christ and on the third day he rose again.

St Paul realised that the message that Christianity has to offer the world is that of the cross of Jesus Christ. In his *First Letter to the Corinthians*, he declared, "We are preaching a crucified Christ: to the Jews an obstacle they cannot get over, to the gentiles foolishness" (*1 Corinthians* 1:23). St Paul realised that the true power of God to save humanity is found in the cross. For him everything else is mere rubbish compared to embracing this power of Christ (*Philippians* 3:8-9). This great act of God is the true liberation of humanity.

St Paul realised that when he preached the crucified Christ the power of God was released. Lives were changed. The cross is the powerful means by which the influence of evil over humanity is broken.

How does this power to save work?

Coming under the redeeming power of the Cross

The sacrifice of Christ, dying on the cross for us, was a definitive act. Mankind was freed from the power of evil, but each person must appropriate into their own lives what Christ has done for them. We need to ensure that what Christ has done for all humanity is made effective in each of our lives personally.

At the most sacred moment of the Mass, immediately after the Consecration, the priest invites the people to proclaim the mystery of faith. The people respond, "We proclaim your Death, O Lord, and profess your Resurrection until you come again." It is a dramatic declaration of the significance of the death of Christ for us. It is a special moment of expressing the heart of our Christian faith and of requesting that we become real beneficiaries of what Christ has done for us on Calvary.

The Christian knows a fundamental truth – we cannot save ourselves. We cannot rely upon ourselves to lead a life worthy enough before God. We are all sinners. We are frail and imperfect human beings. Nothing we can do of ourselves can gain us rightful status before the All Holy God. We are saved in and through Christ.

This is a vital yet difficult concept for contemporary humanity to grasp. We are used to being able to prove our worth. We tend to have a confidence in our ability to meet the challenges of life. We see the triumph of human ability in the great cities we have constructed, in the amazing scientific progress we have made, and in the level of personal sophistication we have achieved through education. Most of us believe we are essentially good and with a little education can be better. This is simply not the case. Our previous consideration of the human condition more accurately presents the truth of the situation. We need to be saved and we cannot save ourselves.

Every Christian places his or her life and eventual salvation under the power of the cross. We surrender ourselves to its saving power. There is a wonderful story told in the Gospels of Jesus walking across the lake to the disciples in the midst of a stormy night. Peter, rather impetuously asks, "Let me come to you across the waters". Jesus says, "Come". Peter begins to walk on the water, but once he becomes aware of the wind and waves he loses confidence and begins to sink. He cries out to the Lord, "save me". Jesus reaches out his hand and draws him out of the water, commenting, "O man of little faith, why did you doubt?" This can be a parable for our lives and ultimately of our death. We have not the power to save ourselves. Relying on the power of Christ we can rise above the forces that can destroy us.

Thus, the conversion moment for each person is when he or she is ready to reach out their hand to Christ and call out, "Save me!" Then the power of Christ becomes the operative force in their lives. We allow ourselves to be saved. This becomes the characteristic attitude of the Christian. A Christian is willing to place his or her life in the hands of God. This becomes a source of freedom and inner peace.

St Paul, as we saw earlier, considered all his status and education as so much "rubbish", desiring only to have "a place in Christ". He came to realise that all which he used to think important in giving value and meaning to his life has no value, all that really counts is the fact that he is "in Christ",[42] that is, his identity and ultimate destiny are bound up in his relationship with Christ.

---

42 Pope Benedict declared 2008-2009 the Year of St Paul. He gave a series of catecheses on St Paul at his Wednesday audiences. On 19 November 2008, he expressed the profound spirit of St Paul in relation to his unity with Christ in these words, "The relationship between Paul and the Risen One is so profound that it impels him to affirm that Christ was not only his life, but his living, to the point that to be able to reach him, even death was a gain (cf. *Philippians* 1:21). It was not because he did not appreciate life, but because he understood that for him, living no longer had another objective; therefore, he no longer had a desire other than to reach Christ, as in an athletic competition, to be with him always. The Risen One had become the beginning and end of his existence, the reason and goal of his running. Only concern for the growth in faith of those he had evangelized and solicitude for all the Churches he had founded (cf. *2 Corinthians* 11:28), induced him to slow down the run toward his only Lord, to wait for his disciples, so that they would be able to run to the goal with him. If in the previous observance of the law he had nothing to reproach himself from the point of view of moral integrity, once overtaken by Christ he preferred not to judge himself (cf. *1 Corinthians* 4:3-4), but limited himself to run to conquer the one who had conquered him (cf. *Philippians* 3:12).

This is the radical nature of being a Christian. It is more than a notional belief in Christ. It cannot be simply contained as a creedal formula. It is something not just of the mind but of the heart. It involves the opening of one's heart and life radically to Christ. It is a realisation that life is to be oriented around Jesus Christ. He is the one and only path and pattern for us.

Pope John Paul II began his pontificate by declaring to the world, "Open the doors to Christ". The words of Pope John Paul deserve quoting as they capture his spirit and the driving motivation of his long and fruitful ministry as Pope:

> Brothers and sisters, do not be afraid to welcome Christ and accept his power. Help the Pope and all those who wish to serve Christ and with Christ's power to serve the human person and the whole of mankind. Do not be afraid. Open wide the doors for Christ. To his saving power open the boundaries of States, economic and political systems, the vast fields of culture, civilization and development. Do not be afraid. Christ knows 'what is in man'. He alone knows it.[43]

---

[43] On Sunday, 22 October 1978, in St Peter's Square during the homily in the Mass for the beginning of his pontificate

4.
A Life in the Holy Spirit

As St John stood before the cross, no doubt lost in confusion and sorrow, he witnessed the soldier taking a lance and piercing the heart of Jesus to ensure that he was in fact dead. This incident had a profound effect on St John.[44] His description of what happened and his subsequent reflection upon it is of great help for us in coming to understand the full implications of the death of Christ for us. It reveals to us as it did to St John the implications of the death of Christ on the cross for us today. We will follow the thought of St John.

St John saw great significance in what he witnessed as he stood before the cross. He saw blood and water flowing from the pierced heart of Jesus. It was as though the final flow of blood from the heart of Christ was followed by a flow of water. In his first letter there is reference to what he calls the "two witnesses", these being the blood and the water (*1 John* 5:5-8). It is an obscure reference on its own, but once we consider his description of what happened on Calvary we gain a clearer picture.

It is a reference to what he described in his Gospel. What John means by "witness" is that the blood and water that flowed from the

---

[44] See *John* 19:31-37. St John was the only one of the evangelist actually present during the crucifixion. He provides some unique material not given by other evangelists. His text alone records the piercing of the heart of Jesus. It is something which John saw as of great significance, as he said, "He who saw this has testified that you may believe. His testimony is true and he knows he speaks the truth". Here the issue for St John is not just the fact that the heart of Jesus was pierced by the soldier's lance, but the fact that blood and water flowed from his pierced side.

heart of Jesus express the nature of the life (and death) of Jesus. Blood is seen as expressive of the sacrifice offered. This is the common Jewish understanding: sacrifices were offered up to God; for example, the blood of bulls at Sinai at the time of the establishing of the Covenant (see *Exodus* 24:8). It is worth commenting at this point about a peculiarly Johannine reference where John the Baptist refers to Jesus as the "lamb of God", that is, the sacrificial lamb (*John* 1:29).

Water is here a reference to the life-giving Spirit. Again the Johannine writings reveal this line of thought. St John writes, "On the last day, the great day of the festival, Jesus stood and cried out: 'Let anyone who is thirsty come to me! Let anyone who believes in me come and drink!'" And then he comments, "As Scripture says, 'From his heart shall flow streams of living water'. He was speaking of the Spirit which those who believed in him were to receive; for there was no Spirit as yet because Jesus had not yet been glorified" (*John* 7:37-39).

Water is equated with the Spirit which has not yet been sent because Jesus has not yet been glorified by dying on the Cross. Thus, for St John, the death of Jesus on the cross is the sacrifice by which the Holy Spirit is released. The full meaning of the death of Jesus becomes clearly evident: it is as though in the flowing forth of the blood and water at Calvary the evangelist (St John) had a moment of personal revelation. At that instant he realised the meaning of what he was witnessing.

St John concludes his account of what he witnessed on Calvary by quoting from the Prophet Zechariah, "They will look to the one whom they have pierced" (*John* 19:37; cf. *Zechariah* 12:10). St John looked up at the cross and saw the pierced heart from which the blood and water flowed. He is encouraging us to do the same. In his Gospel the idea is offered earlier "the Son of Man must be lifted up"[45], that

---

45 See *John* 3:13.

is, Jesus must be crucified ("lifted up") on the cross. This will be the means by which humanity is saved and this will be the means by which the Holy Spirit will be released upon mankind.

Jesus spoke about the intention of God to send the Holy Spirit in a new and all encompassing way into human history upon the completion of his mission. At one point he said that it was necessary for him to go so that the Holy Spirit would be sent.[46] He was signalling that he had a particular mission and that once it was completed God the Father would send forth the Holy Spirit.

This outpouring of the Holy Spirit was realised at Pentecost when the Apostles, gathered in the same room where they had met for the Last Supper, had a profoundly transforming experience. The account of this is found in the *Acts of the Apostles*.[47] St Luke describes how there was a sound of wind outside the house and then there were tongues of fire coming on each of them. Frightened and confused apostles were wonderfully transformed. They found new courage and boldness. We are told that Peter went out on the balcony of the house and began to announce to the crowds that the man they crucified has risen from the dead. After Peter had proclaimed the meaning of the death of Jesus we are told by St Luke that his hearers were "cut to the heart" and asked how they could respond to what Peter had proclaimed. It is then that Peter declares that they must repent and believe and be baptised. This would enable them to receive the Holy Spirit.

This has deep significance for us. The Christian not only embraces faith in Jesus Christ, but expresses this by being baptised. This baptism is not just a ritual act, but a means by which the Holy Spirit is bestowed upon the new believer. Jesus had told his disciples to proclaim the message to all mankind and that they were to baptise, "in the name of the Father and of the Son and of the Holy Spirit" (*Matthew* 28:19).

---

46 See *John* 16:7.
47 See *Acts* 2:1-13.

When a person is baptised they receive the Holy Spirit. They are "born from above" (*John* 3:7). Every baptised Christian receives the gift of the Holy Spirit. They are enabled now to live "a life in the Spirit". The Christian life is a spiritual life, a life lived under the grace and inspiration of the Holy Spirit.

The *Acts of the Apostles* recounts the ways in which the Holy Spirit was active in the lives of the first believers. It speaks, for instance, of the early Christians receiving various spiritual gifts. Peter and John heal a cripple at the temple.[48] St Paul describes some of the ways in which the Holy Spirit was active in the early Christian Communities. He outlines some of the spiritual gifts in his letter to the Corinthians which were obviously manifest in the community in Corinth. He speaks of gifts of preaching and teaching, of prophesy and healing and the gift of tongues.[49]

The Scriptures and the tradition of the Church witness to the gifts of the Holy Spirit, but the important thing is the indwelling presence of the Holy Spirit assisting us in living the Christian life. The indwelling of the Holy Spirit means that the Christian lives at this level of the spiritual. We live a spiritual life because God's own life is within us. God's Spirit is within us transforming our lives. The Christian lives a life of Grace.

Christian understanding of the nature of human life

In order to consider how we can develop a Christian character we must clearly grasp the nature of the human person. We can summarise the above by saying that the human person is created ("very good"), fallen (prone to temptation and afflictions) and redeemed (saved and empowered by the Holy Spirit). With this foundational understanding we can now move to consider how we can form a solid Christian character.

---

[48] See *Acts* 3:1-10.
[49] See *1 Corinthians* 12:4-11.

Part 2

Christian Character

1.
The Pursuit of Virtue

How do we form character? Some would argue that we are largely the product of our experiences, good and bad. This is to view the human person more as a passive recipient of forces that bear in upon us. There is much debate about "nature or nurture" – are we the product of our genes or the result of the way we have been brought up? This suggests that our character is somehow determined by influences beyond our control. We are shaped by all sorts of random circumstances. This is a bleak picture of human life.

The human person is not just moulded by external forces. The human person is an acting agent possessing freedom and capable of making choices. We become, in fact, the product of our choices. Character is built upon the foundation of decisions that we make in response to situations in which we find ourselves. Character is the fruit of our decision to take responsibility for our lives. We choose what we become.

However we do not simply construct ourselves from our own efforts. As we have considered above, God has acted in human history to release a power to transform human life. We speak of Grace – the action of the Holy Spirit in our lives. So we use our freedom – we make choices – and God offers his Grace – the power of the Holy Spirit – to assist us.

One of the most crucial of our decisions is whether or not we allow God to act in our lives. We can try to construct ourselves relying upon our own powers, or we can entrust ourselves to God and allow God the space and opportunity to help us grow and be formed in character.

The second part of this book will examine how we can enable this to happen. It will examine the path of virtue.

The meaning of Virtue

What is virtue? The classical Greek philosophers developed the notion of virtue. As we have seen the early Christian Fathers took up the notion and gave it a place in their spiritual and moral teaching. The Greeks spoke of moral virtues. Christian thinkers called them human virtues, or natural virtues. The Fathers also identified divine or supernatural virtues which came to be called the theological virtues. In our consideration of developing character on a day to day basis we will principally concentrate on the human virtues. These are basic virtues that are reflected in our human character.

The Greek poet, Pindar, defined the main human virtues as prudence, justice, courage and self-control. Plato and Aristotle wrote on these virtues. Aristotle said that virtue comes about as a result of habit.[50] As we have seen, virtues are dispositions to act in certain ways in response to similar situations, practices of behaving in a certain way. Thus, good conduct arises from habits that in turn can only be acquired by repeated action and correction, making the growth in moral character an intensely practical discipline.

Behaving in a particular way, for example being courageous, will eventually lead us to possessing the virtue of courage. The more a virtue is practiced the more it becomes a part of character.

Virtue is in fact the enhancement of the human character so that we become who we should be. Virtue can simply be an admirable quality in a person. Good citizenship expressed through service to the country or humanity can be seen as a virtue and is indeed acknowledged through civil awards, like the Noble Peace Prize or the Order of Australia.

---

50 In Book II of Nicomachean Ethics, Aristotle states that "moral excellence [i.e., virtue] comes about as a result of habit" (1103a16-17).

Here, in our context, we are speaking more of virtue as a moral quality. The pursuit of virtue as a moral quality is the path for human personal growth: the development of character. The pursuit of virtue is simply the choice to pursue that which is good.

The word, virtue, is not found significantly in the Scriptures, though St Peter has a reference in his Second Letter which reflects our theme: "add virtue to your faith" (*2 Peter* 1:5). In the teaching of Jesus there are references to walking the path of virtue, though the word "virtue" is not specifically used. For instance, he speaks of the "narrow path" that leads to life (*Matthew* 7:13).

The New Testament writers speak on a number of occasions of various vices to avoid and virtues to cultivate. In his *Letter to the Galatians*, St Paul writes:

> When self-indulgence is at work the results are obvious: sexual vice, impurity, and sensuality, the worship of false gods and sorcery; antagonisms and rivalry, jealousy, bad temper and quarrels, disagreements, factions and malice, drunkenness, orgies and all such things. And about these, I tell you now as I have told you in the past, that people who behave in these ways will not inherit the kingdom of God. On the other hand the fruit of the Spirit is love, joy, peace, patience, kindness, goodness, trustfulness, gentleness and self-control; no law can touch such things as these. (5:19-23).

Simply, St Paul is saying that a Christian living under the influence of the Holy Spirit and desiring to live in imitation of Christ will grow in virtue. In his *Letter to the Philippians*, St Paul says:

> ... let your minds be filled with everything that is true, everything that is honourable, everything that is upright and pure, everything that we love and admire -- with whatever is good and praiseworthy (4:8).

This is the attitude of the Christian. We pursue what we see as the good.

Thus, the *Catechism of the Catholic Church* describes virtue as "an habitual and firm disposition to do the good. It allows the person not only to perform good acts, but to give the best of himself". It adds, "The virtuous person tends toward the good with all his sensory and spiritual powers; he pursues the good and chooses it in concrete actions."[51]

Virtue is steadfastness and facility in doing good, springing from the heart of the person. Again we follow the Catholic Catechism in its description of the essence of virtue.

> Human virtues are firm attitudes, stable dispositions, habitual perfections of intellect and will that govern our actions, order our passions, and guide our conduct according to reason and faith. They make possible ease, self-mastery, and joy in leading a morally good life. The virtuous man is he who freely practices the good. The moral virtues are acquired by human effort. They are the fruit and seed of morally good acts; they dispose all the powers of the human being for communion with divine love.[52]

Thus, we choose to be virtuous. We decide to follow a path that will enable us to grow in virtue. One figure in the Catholic tradition who understood this particularly is St Benedict, responsible for the establishing of a rule of life for monks that would be the predominant pattern for monastic life in the Western Church. St Benedict says that a monk will grow in Christ-likeness as he pursues a pattern of virtue and that the end result will be one who has "good habit and delight in virtue"[53].

In the matter of personal decision, it is worth noting that before a person is baptised they are asked a three-fold question: "do you reject Satan, and all his works and all his empty promises". This question requires the person to engage in a personal decision to reject evil and

---

51 *Catechism of the Catholic Church*, n. 1803.

52 *Catechism of the Catholic Church*, n. 1804.

53 *Rule of St Benedict*, Ch. 7, v. 70.

choose good. This must be the ongoing pattern for Christian growth in virtue.

The Fathers of the Church spoke of the virtues. Saint Cyril of Alexandria expresses the growth in the Christian life in these words, Christ "forms us according to his image, in such a way that the traits of his divine nature shine forth in us through sanctification and justice and the life which is good and in conformity with virtue... The beauty of this image shines forth in us who are in Christ, when we show ourselves to be good in our works."[54] This is what the growth in virtue seeks to achieve, simply that we reflect more and more the character of Christ.

St Gregory Nazianzus notes that "God is called love and peace and by these names he urges us to become transformed according to the virtues that qualify him."[55] He comments, using a notion that the Fathers of the East particularly liked, that the virtues are a measure of our deification.[56]

Our immediate sense of walking the path of virtue is that it will be a challenge and a hard way. But this pursuit of virtue has, as the saying goes, "its own reward". St Antony of Egypt, the Father of Monasticism, commented, "Virtue is not far from us, nor is it without ourselves, but it is within us, and is easy if only we are willing."[57] As we begin to walk the path of virtue it is indeed hard, but as we progress it becomes easier, even a joy. Just as when we commence any task, like learning the piano, it is difficult at the beginning but becomes easier – and a joy – as we progress; so it is with virtue.

---

[54] *Tractatus ad Tiberium Diaconum sociosque*, II. *Responsiones ad Tiberium Diaconum sociosque*: Saint Cyril of Alexandria, *In Divi Johannis Evangelium*, vol. III, ed. Philip Edward Pusey, Brussels, Culture et Civilisation (1965), 590. Quoted in *Veritatis Splendor*, n. 73.

[55] *Carminum Liber* I.II.7.

[56] *Oratio* 6,12.

[57] *Life of Antony*, 20.

Human Virtues and Theological Virtues

As we noted in traditional Catholic thought virtues are either "human" or "theological". The human virtues are those that are exercised in our daily living. They are basic dispositions that we adopt showing a self mastery which is reflected in a morally – and humanly – good life. These virtues are the product of effort on our part to foster them. In this area are the four "cardinal" virtues which ancient Greek thought has identified: prudence, justice, fortitude and temperance. Around these four key virtues are clustered other virtues. A person grows in the human virtues by firstly learning of them. Education in what virtues are is the beginning of recognising them and their value in enhancing human life. Then the person must by choice and perseverance, foster them. However in this process it is not only the human effort that is important. As we have seen the decision to pursue a virtuous life is aided by the action of Grace. The Christian life is a life lived under the guidance and assistance of the Holy Spirit. The desire to grow in virtue is then aided by the action of the Holy Spirit.[58]

The theological virtues are seen as those that directly relate a person to their life in God. These are three: faith, hope and charity. In living a life of faith a person is further imbued with virtues that flow from their inner spiritual life. Faith, hope and love are virtues expressed in human life but they have a spiritual or divine source. They are more immediately the fruit of the presence and activity of the Holy Spirit. But like the human virtues they, too, need to be desired and cultivated. The nurturing of these theological virtues is found in the quality of the inner life "in God" of the person.

We will now consider a range of virtues that mark the character of a Christian. In our approach we will not follow the traditional divisions as outlined above. Rather we will seek to look at the building of a

---

[58] See *Catechism of the Catholic Church*, nn. 1810-1811.

sound Christian character on the basis of key dispositions which are proposed in the Sacred Scriptures and in the living tradition of the Church as the building blocks of the Christian life. While we don't master one virtue and then advance to the next, some virtues are necessary as a foundation upon which other virtues will be able to flourish. This is the approach we will be taking.

To begin with we will examine the question of self discipline without which growth in virtue is not possible.

2.
The Disciplined Life: Asceticism

We live in an era and in a society where there is much interest in sport. We highly respect those sportsmen and women who achieve in their respective fields. They are celebrated and rewarded financially. We appreciate achievement in sport. While we don't necessarily dwell on it, we know that anyone who has reached the peak of their sport has had to devote extraordinary effort and dedication. A person may have a certain aptitude or natural gifts in a particular sport, but talent by itself is not enough.

We can consider all sorts of sports, but let us consider swimmers. They must spend years rising before dawn and doing endless laps of the pool. They are coached. They watch what they eat. They are totally focussed on achieving their goals. Without an extraordinary level of personal dedication they will not achieve the results they hope for. In so many aspects of life final achievement is the result of years of dedicated effort. Those who achieve have moments of personal triumph, but the hidden years of toil and sacrifice are what have enabled them to achieve their goals.

Referring to swimmers again, they speak about their "PB" – their personal best. They are focussed upon improving themselves, of achieving their potential. In one sense they are always competing against themselves. They are always trying to better their previous best. Anyone desiring to grow in virtue likewise has to embrace a path of self discipline in the same way that an athlete does.

From Stoicism to Asceticism

In ancient Greek society the response to widespread moral laxity was the philosophy of Stoicism. The Stoic proposed that an application of right-thinking and rigorous self-discipline would strengthen the will to overcome the passions and ultimately achieve a state of inner calm and serenity. Stoics were materialists – they did not believe in the existence of the soul after death.

Early Christian writers were influenced by Stoicism, though saw limits in this philosophy. They developed a Christian concept of self-discipline, calling it *asceticism*. The word comes from the Greek, *askesis*, which means training, exercise, or practice. There is a parallel here with sport. St Paul used the image of the athlete to speak of the discipline required of a Christian. He tells us, "Do you not realise that, though all the runners in the stadium take part in the race, only one of them gets the prize? Run like that – to win. Every athlete concentrates completely on training, and this is to win a wreath that will wither, whereas ours will never wither. So that is how I run, not without a clear goal; and how I box, not wasting blows on air. I punish my body and bring it under control, to avoid any risk that, having acted as herald for others, I myself may be disqualified" (*1 Corinthians* 9:24-27).

The Christian notion of asceticism, however, should not be viewed simply as the application of physical disciplines. Asceticism is ethical in nature and has to do with growth in virtue. The key to recognising the meaning of Christian asceticism is that it is directed towards God. An athlete may be very ascetical in the way he eats, his firm routines, his abstinence, but these are to achieve athletic prowess. A person may be very abstemious when it comes to food and drink because of their job, or for health reasons. For all sorts of reasons which may have nothing to do with growth in virtue, people are ascetical. They diet, they have exercise routines, they may choose to be vegetarian. All of this is for self improvement. Christian asceticism has as its goal ultimately the love of God.

Religious Asceticism

Asceticism has been a part of all major religious movements. Jewish asceticism was associated with the schools of prophets and the Nazarites.

The asceticism among the Brahmins of India is intended to inculcate the virtues of truthfulness, honesty, self-control, obedience, temperance, alms-giving, care of the sick, meekness, forgiveness of injuries, returning good for evil, etc. Brahmin teaching forbids suicide, abortion, perjury, slander, drunkenness, gluttony, usury, hypocrisy, slothfulness, and cruelty to animals. Ten vows bind the Brahmin to the practice of these virtues. Its practice of penance is extraordinary. Besides what is left to personal initiative, the Laws of Manu decree that the Brahmin should embrace some rigorous physical austerities, like standing in the snow in wet clothing.

For the Buddhists, there are five great duties: not to kill any living creature, not to steal, not to act unchastely, not to lie, not to drink intoxicating liquor. The eight-fold path of virtues is: right beliefs, right aspiration, right speech, right conduct, right means of livelihood, right endeavour, right memory, right meditation. The cultivation of meekness, both internal and external, is expressly inculcated. In the monasteries, confession of faults, but only of external ones, is practised, and great importance is attached to meditation. Their penances are comparatively moderate.

Religious asceticism is open to heretical extremes. Christianity has not been free of some heretical tendencies. For instance, in the second century there were a group of heretical Gnostics, chiefly Syrians, who called themselves the Encratites, or The Austere. Because of their erroneous views about matter, they withdrew from all contact with the world, and denounced marriage as impure. About the same period the Montanists forbade second marriage, enjoined rigorous fasts, insisted on the perpetual exclusion from the Church of those who had ever committed grievous sin, stigmatized flight in time of persecution as reprehensible, protested that virgins should be always veiled, reprobated paintings, statuary, military service, theatres, and all worldly sciences.

In the third century the Manichaens held marriage to be unlawful and refrained from wine, meat, milk, and eggs; all of which did not deter them from the grossest immorality. The Cathari of the twelfth century were puritans, as the Greek origin of their name (*katharos* meaning pure) indicates. Though teaching the doctrines of the Manichaeans, they affected to live a purer life than the rest of the Church.

In a religious setting a sound understanding of the role of asceticism is very important. Let us for a moment consider the Christian tradition.

Renouncing of self

As we saw, the word "asceticism" comes from the Greek word meaning to exercise or to train. In the Christian context we are speaking of training in Christian living. It is the ordering of our life so that we grow in Christian virtue. The starting point for this may appear negative, but it is the necessary point from which to advance.

In ancient times when an adult was baptised the candidate would approach a baptismal pool, go down three steps, be baptised and rise up. To be baptised they would remove their old garments and put on a new baptismal robe. This graphically illustrated the idea that the Christian chooses to leave behind an old life "in the world" and "put on Christ"[59]. The Christian choses to live a new life and to do this renounces a life lived for this world alone.

St John writes, "Do not love the world or what is in the world. If anyone does love the world, the love of the Father finds no place in him, because everything there is in the world – disordered bodily desires, disordered desires of the eyes, pride in possession – is not from the Father but is from the world. And the world, with all its

---

[59] *Romans* 13:14 says, "Instead, clothe yourselves with the Lord Jesus, and do not obey your flesh and its desires".

disordered desires, is passing away. But whoever does the will of God remains for ever" (*1 John* 2:15-17).

This and other texts of Scripture have given rise to Christian writings that concern the need to renounce the world. An example of this is the letter of Eucherius, Bishop of Lyons, to Valerianus, a philosopher.[60] It is a call to faith and it urges the philosopher to embrace the Christian Way rather than that of a worldly philosophy. Eucharius concludes his treatise by a final exhortation:

> Take up your eyes from the Earth and look about you, my most dear Valerian; spread forth your sails, and hasten from this stormy sea of secular negotiations, into the calm and secure harbour of Christian religion. This is the only haven into which we all drive from the raging surges of this malicious world. This is our shelter from the loud and persecuting whirlwinds of Time. Here is our sure station and certain rest; here a large and silent recess, secluded from the world, opens and offers itself unto us. Here a pleasant, serene tranquillity shines upon us. Hither, when you are come, your weather-beaten vessel - after all your fruitless toils - shall at last find rest, and securely ride at anchor of the Cross.

This notion of renunciation of the world goes even further, because it must also involve a renunciation of self. The Lord taught, "If anyone wants to be a follower of mine, let him renounce himself and take up his cross and follow me" (*Matthew* 16:24). This can seem a hard saying to many today. What did Jesus mean when He said that, to be His disciples, we must deny ourselves, take up our cross, and follow Him? The context of this saying is that Jesus had been predicting His death. Peter challenged Him, and Jesus responded strongly to Peter. Then Jesus made this statement. Jesus was speaking about his coming death. Peter had reacted to this idea. So Jesus says that we must learn to deny our natural intentions and desires if we wish to be true disciples.

---

[60] Eucherius was born in the latter half of the fourth century; died about 449AD. He was chosen Bishop of Lyons probably in 434AD.

Denying self requires us to be willing to give up anything that we might want or seek that would hinder us in doing the will of God. This does not mean that, if we want something, it is necessarily wrong. It means we must take our wants and desires down from the focus of our life and place Jesus and His will as the governing power in our lives. There is room in each life for only one master (*Matthew* 6:19-24). If God is to be the centre of our lives, then our will must be made subservient to His. We must be willing to give up anything in life in order to please God.[61] For the Christian there is a need to walk a path of self renunciation. For Catholics this notion is captured particularly during the Season of Lent. We engage in some practices of self denial. There is a need for some physical expression of self renunciation, but this is, if you like, training, for the real self renunciation is at the inner level – the level of the will. We will give this more attention later.

Is this emphasis on asceticism a negative approach to life? Our Christian concept of the world and of ourselves is grounded in the Genesis accounts of creation which declare that all that God has made is "good". It is not a rejection of the created world per se. Nor is it an expression of a dualism found in many heretical spiritual movements over history. It is the recognition of the reality and effects of the Original Sin of Adam and Eve. It is contrasting "spirit and flesh", "light and darkness", the "outer and inner man", "God and the world", presented in the Gospels, especially St John, and the Pauline epistles. It deals with that part of reality which is marred by sin and is inimical to our salvation.

Human nature, because of the Fall, suffers under concupiscence.[62] We readily recognise our tendency to sin. As we have seen, temptation

---

61 See *Romans* 12:1,2; *Matthew* 6:33; *Luke* 14:25-33; *2 Corinthians* 5:14,15.

62 Concupiscence is selfish human desire for an object, person, or experience. It is the orientation of our fallen human nature to long for fleshly appetites, often associated with a desire to do things which are proscribed.

is described as coming from the world, the Devil and the flesh. We all know of the power of the "flesh" – we are driven by a lust for physical pleasure and self-gratification. We all need self-discipline.

Fasting

Catholics are familiar with the call to fasting during Lent, though often are not aware of the expectation that they should exercise some act of self denial each Friday.[63] Pope Benedict XVI spoke of fasting in his Lenten message for 2009. He said, "We might wonder what value and meaning there is for us Christians in depriving ourselves of something that in itself is good and useful for our bodily sustenance". Indeed Catholics do wonder about the value of fasting. It seems old fashioned. Yet fasting is a practice enshrined in the Scriptures, both in the Old and New Testaments. Indeed, there are too many references to mention. We are aware of the Lord himself choosing to spend forty days in the desert in prayer and fasting after his baptism in the Jordan and before commencing his public ministry.

The Pope comments that, "In our own day, fasting seems to have lost something of its spiritual meaning, and has taken on, in a culture characterized by the search for material well-being, a therapeutic value for the care of one's body. Fasting certainly brings benefits to physical

---

[63] The *Code of Canon Law* indicates that Catholics are supposed to abstain from meat on all Fridays during the year. Canon 1250 states "All Fridays through the year and the time of Lent are penitential days and times throughout the universal Church". The following canon adds, "Abstinence from eating meat or another food according to the prescriptions of the conference of bishops is to be observed on Fridays throughout the year, unless they are solemnities; abstinence and fast are to be observed on Ash Wednesday and on the Friday of the Passion and Death of Our Lord Jesus Christ. Canon 1253 then comments, "It is for the conference of bishops to determine more precisely the observance of fast and abstinence and to substitute in whole or in part for fast and abstinence other forms of penance, especially works of charity and exercises of piety".

well-being, but for believers, it is, in the first place, a "therapy" to heal all that prevents them from conformity to the will of God". Discussion of diets fills magazines, and many today willingly undertake all sorts of restrictions in what they eat for reasons of physical health or body image, but as the Pope mentions these are for human purposes. Christians undertake acts of fasting for a spiritual purpose.

The Pope comments on some of the spiritual fruits that can result from fasting. He says, "Fasting represents an important ascetical practice, a spiritual arm to do battle against every possible disordered attachment to ourselves. Freely chosen detachment from the pleasure of food and other material goods helps the disciple of Christ to control the appetites of nature, weakened by original sin, whose negative effects impact the entire human person". The practice of fasting is part of the asceticism which should mark the life of every Christian.

Pleasure and pain

A problem for every human being is the need to control our love of bodily pleasure and our fear of bodily pain. We are a complex of biological drives and human needs. These are to be harmonised and focused through the action of the will. In other words, we need to make decisions about how we approach issues of pleasure and pain.

The pleasure of the bodily senses is not wrong. It is a natural thing: 'No one can live without some bodily, sense pleasure" (Aristotle). The exaggerated seeking of sensual pleasure, though, gives way to hedonism.[64] The desire for pleasure must be kept in control. For example, sexual pleasure should not be pursued as an end unto itself. Sexual pleasure finds in full meaning within marriage. This is one of the issues that we face in our culture. There is a desire to be free from any constraints. Individual freedom is seen as a personal right. Many

---

[64] The word hedonism derives from the Greek word for "delight" ἡδονισμός hēdonismos. As a theory it argues that pleasure is the only intrinsic good. A hedonist strives to maximize pleasure and minimise pain.

would argue that we should be able to do "one's own thing". There is a resistance to being denied the pursuit of pleasure.

At the same time Christianity does not favour a grim asceticism like that of the Jansenists[65] or Puritans[66] who consider human life completely corrupted by the Fall. The Catholic Catechism[67] states simply that asceticism has a place in the Christian life: "The way of perfection passes by way of the Cross. There is no holiness without renunciation and spiritual battle. Spiritual progress entails the ascesis and mortification that gradually lead to living in the peace and joy of the Beatitudes".

Every person experiences trials in life. They may be minor – failing to get the hoped for job – or major – a serious illness or some tragedy. Such experiences cause us to question: why me? There is no immediate answer to this question. The Christian, however, can approach this question from a position of faith. From the wisdom literature of the Old Testament comes the line: "My child, do not scorn correction from Yahweh, do not resent his reproof; for Yahweh reproves those he loves, as a father the child whom he loves." (*Proverbs* 3:11-12). The Lord disciplines those he loves, as a father does his son. We can see a truth here - we all need some discipline for our own good. Another scriptural image that is appropriate here is the reference of the Lord to the necessity to prune the vine. It is found in *John* 15:2 – "Every

---

[65] Jansenism was a religious movement in France which took its name from the theologian Jansenius (Cornelius Jansen, 1585-1638). He taught a strict spirituality that held that human beings cannot achieve goodness without the intervention of God's grace and that only a minority of individuals have been predestined by God for salvation. It spread in France in the seventeenth century and was condemned by the Church.

[66] Puritanism existed in 16th and 17th century England and included a number of religious groups advocating for more "purity" of worship and doctrine, as well as personal and group piety. Puritans felt that the English Reformation had not gone far enough, and that the Church of England was tolerant of practices which they associated with the Catholic Church.

[67] *Catechism of the Catholic Church*, n. 2015.

branch in me that bears no fruit he cuts away, and every branch that does bear fruit he prunes to make it bear even more." One other Scriptural passage that offers a Christian perspective is found in the *Letter to the Hebrews*:

> Have you forgotten that encouraging text in which you are addressed as sons? My son, do not scorn correction from the Lord, do not resent his training, for the Lord trains those he loves, and chastises every son he accepts. Perseverance is part of your training; God is treating you as his sons. Has there ever been any son whose father did not train him? If you were not getting this training, as all of you are, then you would be not sons but bastards. Besides, we have all had our human fathers who punished us, and we respected them for it; all the more readily ought we to submit to the Father of spirits, and so earn life. Our human fathers were training us for a short life and according to their own lights; but he does it all for our own good, so that we may share his own holiness. Of course, any discipline is at the time a matter for grief, not joy; but later, in those who have undergone it, it bears fruit in peace and uprightness. So steady all weary hands and trembling knees and make your crooked paths straight; then the injured limb will not be maimed, it will get better instead. (*Hebrews* 12:5-13)

One final reference from Scripture on this theme is found in the opening of the *First Letter of St Peter*:

> This is a great joy to you, even though for a short time yet you must bear all sorts of trials; so that the worth of your faith, more valuable than gold, which is perishable even if it has been tested by fire, may be proved -- to your praise and honour when Jesus Christ is revealed. You have not seen him, yet you love him; and still without seeing him you believe in him and so are already filled with a joy so glorious that it cannot be described; and you are sure of the goal of your faith, that is, the salvation of your souls. (*1 Peter* 1:6-9)

These texts invite us to consider our experiences of suffering in the light of faith. Trials and suffering can in fact become sources of the purification of our personality and the strengthening of our character. It is true that we all need to be purified in our attitudes. We know that when all is going well for us we can feel invincible. There is a wonderful insight found in *Psalm* 30: "Carefree, I used to think, 'Nothing can ever shake me!' Your favour, Yahweh, set me on impregnable heights, but you turned away your face and I was terrified." It is true that when things are going well we can become full of ourselves, we need to be brought down to earth.

Trials can be the making of us. They strengthen our resolve. They purify our motives. They give us a realistic view of life and of ourselves. Trials can be keys to personal growth.

A Note on Spiritual Purification

Classic Catholic Spiritual Theology speaks of the process of purification associated with a growth in prayer. The Carmelite teaching (Saints Teresa of Avila and John of the Cross) speaks of a purification of the external senses which require a moving away from the pursuit of even lawful pleasures and the practice of bodily self denial. Then comes the process of the purification of the internal senses – imagination, memory. There follows the purification of the passions, then the intellect and finally the will.[68] Spiritual writers speak of the fact that the believer upon entering into the spiritual life experiences blessings – joy, peace, a sense of the presence of God, but then in order to grow the young Christian must be stripped of an attachment to comforting spiritual feelings. The Lord seems to become absent. Prayer dries up. This, however, is a path to growth and maturity. We will consider this in more detail when we address questions of the spiritual life.

---

[68] A very good description of this can be found in *Spiritual Theology* by Jordan Aumann.

The Companion Virtues: Moderation and Self Control

The virtue of asceticism or self discipline which we have been examining has two important companion virtues – moderation and self control. The saying attributed to the Roman poet, Horace, "In medio stat virtus" – Virtue stands in the middle – expresses the importance of moderation. Virtue is in the moderate, not in the extreme, position.

Moderation can be as simple as maintaining a balance and having common sense in approaching disciplines. We can note that it is easy to become extreme in acts of self discipline. Excessive dieting can lead to malnutrition. The athlete must ensure that a healthy balance is preserved in exercises. Excessive training can harm their performance and even be dangerous.

In this area of self discipline the danger of excess is always there. It is useful to have a mentor, just as an athlete has a trainer. In the Christian tradition the practice of having a spiritual director is a healthy approach to managing a sound Christian growth.

The Wisdom of St John of the Cross

We previously mentioned the teaching of St John of the Cross. From his book, *Ascent of Mount Carmel* comes the following.[69]

> Strive always to prefer, not that which is easiest, but that which is most difficult;
>
> Not that which is most delectable, but that which is most unpleasing;
>
> Not that which gives most pleasure, but rather that which gives least;
>
> Not that which is restful, but that which is wearisome;
>
> Not that which is consolation, but rather that which is disconsolateness;

---

69 St John of the Cross, *Ascent of Mount Carmel, Book 1, Chapter 13.*

Not that which is greatest, but that which is least;

Not that which is loftiest and most precious, but that which is lowest and most despised;

Not that which is a desire for anything, but that which is a desire for nothing;

Strive to go about seeking not the best of temporal things, but the worst.

Strive thus to desire to enter into complete detachment and emptiness and poverty, with respect to everything that is in the world, for Christ's sake.

3.
A Foundational Virtue – Humility

What is the quality upon which a sound character can be built? To answer this question we will consider the thought of St Benedict of Nursia – the father of Western Monasticism. His Rule has shaped the lives of thousands of monks over a millennia and a half. The virtue that receives particular attention from St Benedict is that of humility. In the light of his experience of establishing common life for monks, it was clear that the vital ingredient for a monk to advance in human and Christian character is the embrace of the virtue of humility.

Would we consider this as the key to developing character? It seems such a foreign concept in the contemporary world which emphasises self assertion and individual rights. Indeed our culture is built around the right of the individual to self fulfilment.

Let us consider the place of humility in every human life. A humble person is someone who is an attractive person. We are drawn towards them. A proud and arrogant person repulses us. A humble person is one who accepts him or herself, conscious of both their strengths and their weaknesses. A humble person does not attempt to inflate their importance. They do not see themselves in competition with others. It is the humble person who was the subject of the teaching of Jesus given in the Beatitudes – "Blessed are the poor in spirit" (*Matthew* 5:3). It is a common theme in the teaching of Jesus, attesting to his own appreciation of the importance of this virtue.[70]

---

[70] There are many texts in the Gospels where Christ explicitly refers to humility. This highlights the fact that humility was a very important virtue in his mind. See such texts as *John* 13:1-17; *Matthew* 16:24; 20:16; 26-28; *Luke* 14:11.

Yet today humility is approached with scepticism. It is not a virtue popularly promoted, even in some Christian circles. The world around us has reservations about it. Many would view humility as a negative characteristic in a person. There is a reaction to lingering Jansenism[71] which plagued the Church for several centuries. Jansenism promoted a notion of humility that carried with it self-condemnation. Today people long to take a positive spirit of life and the good of the human person. Today the attribute of God most advanced is that of love and mercy. People reject a view that God is a god of judgement and condemnation.

Some of the concerns about humility may be expressed thus:

- Does it promote passivity? Is humility connected with an intense introspection? Does it foster excessive scruples in dwelling on faults and failures?
- Does humility lead to blandness? Humility fosters the notion that a person is not allowed to be assertive, outgoing, adventurous.
- Is humility simply low self esteem?
- Can it promote too much "gravitas" – seriousness, a sense of worthlessness which can lead to a lack of initiative?
- Some can fear that it is a tool of authority in order to foster compliance. It can result in mediocrity. There is the concern that authority could use the promotion of humility to subjugate individuals.

These are some of the questions that people have whereby they are doubtful about the value of developing this virtue. We will need to consider these objections.

---

[71] Jansenism was an heretical doctrine proposed by a Dutch theologian Cornelis Jansen (1585-1638). It was prevalent in the Church during the 17th and 18th centuries. It denied the freedom of the will. It emphasized puritanical moral attitudes.

Humility as Truth

Erasmus, Dutch priest and humanist (16th century) stated simply: "Humility is Truth". This is the key to appreciating the real nature and value of this virtue. The word, humility, comes from the Latin word, "humus" – the ground. It reminds us that we were created from the earth. This is our true nature as human beings. It is a virtue by which a person knows himself as he truly is. St Thomas Aquinas teaches: "The virtue of humility consists in keeping oneself within one's own bounds, not reaching out to things above one."[72] Thus humility is to live true to one's nature.

In considering our true place we can say firstly that we are not gods. This was the temptation in the Garden of Eden – to become as God. Pride was the first sin. The sin was to deny our true nature and avoid facing our vulnerability, weakness and the limitations of our human condition. We are creatures and thus depend on God. A fundamental submission to God is critical in order to assume our rightful place. Thus we are created to worship and obey God. We, as human beings, are flawed. Catholic teaching on Original Sin is important here. Concupiscence, as we have seen, is the daily human reality. Each of us has a personal history of sin. Each of us has rejected the good, the true, and the beautiful. We have turned from God. We all have fundamental limits to our humanity. We are imperfect. The older we are the more our personal history reveals the serious limits to our character. We do not simply advance from the good to the better. Life reveals the deep darkness that haunts our growth.

However, all of this is not to foster an essential pessimism about ourselves – the human race is not a *massa damnata* (condemned people). The Christian message is about salvation, about grace, about transformation and finally about Beatitude. But the truth remains - we human beings are flawed and subject to sin. Humility is about

---

[72] *Summa Contra Gent.*, Bk. IV, Ch. lv.

facing the truth about ourselves and being neither overly optimistic, nor unnecessarily pessimistic. It is about being real about ourselves. Humility grounds us. It gives us the true foundation upon which to build our Christian life. Humility also unites us in the human race – in solidarity with others. Thus we move to compassion and to communion with others. Humility doesn't mean denying our gifts – but in recognising them and acknowledging their source.

Humility enables us to be our real selves – that is, without artifice (the hypocrite is the one with the mask). Being our true selves thus enables each one to find an inner peace and a true happiness. It is not the case that the sinner has the good time, while the believer is being miserably good – the unbridled pursuit of pleasure is in the end unsatisfying. The humble person is the one who is finally satisfied – "Blessed are the poor in spirit, theirs is the Kingdom of heaven."

1. The Teaching of Jesus Christ

Humility, as we have said, was a significant aspect of the teaching of the Lord. There are many examples. In *Matthew* 18:4, Jesus teaches, "the one who makes himself as little as this little child is the greatest in the kingdom of Heaven." Many times the Lord speaks about adopting the attitude of a servant (and not a master): "Among you this is not to happen. No; anyone who wants to become great among you must be your servant, and anyone who wants to be first among you must be slave to all" (*Mark* 10:43-44). On another occasion Jesus teaches:

> 'When someone invites you to a wedding feast, do not take your seat in the place of honour. A more distinguished person than you may have been invited, and the person who invited you both may come and say, "Give up your place to this man." And then, to your embarrassment, you will have to go and take the lowest place. No; when you are a guest, make your way to the lowest place and sit there, so that, when your host comes, he may say, "My friend, move up higher." Then, everyone with you at the table will see you honoured. For everyone who raises himself

up will be humbled, and the one who humbles himself will be raised up.' (*Luke* 14:8-11)

One short parable that captures a comparison between the self righteous (proud) religious person and a person who is conscious of their unworthiness before God is the parable of the two men who go up to the temple to pray:

> 'Two men went up to the Temple to pray, one a Pharisee, the other a tax collector. The Pharisee stood there and said this prayer to himself, "I thank you, God, that I am not grasping, unjust, adulterous like everyone else, and particularly that I am not like this tax collector here. I fast twice a week; I pay tithes on all I get." The tax collector stood some distance away, not daring even to raise his eyes to heaven; but he beat his breast and said, "God, be merciful to me, a sinner." This man, I tell you, went home again justified; the other did not. For everyone who raises himself up will be humbled, but anyone who humbles himself will be raised up.' (*Luke* 18:10-14)

It is clear from these examples that the Lord considered humility a vital virtue for his disciples. His own witness of mixing with the poor and with those who were known as sinners revealed his own inner spirit. He was born in a stable, was content to be among ordinary folk and saw himself as a servant to all. Jesus who was Son of God is the great model for us.

2. Humility in the Teaching of St Benedict

A classical treatment of the virtue of humility is found in the Rule of St Benedict. More precisely it is found in Chapter 7 of the Rule and comprises of seventy verses. St Benedict proposes twelve steps of humility in a ladder whose goal is perfect love. The Rule outlines stages in the growth into humility. They are part of what Benedict sees as the "school of God's service"[73]. The Rule, it must be noted, clearly

---

[73] In the prologue to the Rule, St Benedict uses this phrase to describe what the pattern of monastic life seeks to achieve.

states that there is to be "nothing harsh or heavy". Benedict, in the end, considers humility as the key to monastic living. Or to put it another way: humility is the key to true Christian growth. Humility opens the doors to the true formation of character.

Fr Michael Casey, a monk of the Trappist Monastery at Tarrawarra in Victoria, has written on St Benedict's teaching in his book, *Truthful Living,* and there he analyses and puts into a modern context this teaching of St Benedict. I will follow the thought of Fr Casey.

St Benedict begins by reminding the monk that it is God who exalts. He quotes Christ's teaching: "Everyone who exalts himself shall be humbled, and he who humbles himself shall be exalted" (*Luke* 14:11). He then proposes a ladder to ascend towards God. This ladder is the cultivation of the virtue of humility.

Moving to consider the first step, Casey categorises it as a call to seriousness. St Benedict teaches, "The first degree of humility, then, is that a person keep the fear of God before his eyes and beware of ever forgetting it". He adds, "Let a man consider that God is always looking at him from heaven, that his actions are everywhere visible to the divine eyes." Casey proposes "seriousness" as the opposite of frivolity. Frivolity, the pursuit of fun, a mindless interest in pleasure, militates against any spiritual growth. Conversion is a "coming to one's senses". It is the abandoning of mindlessness. The process of basic Christian growth is one of a transition to a careful, industrious and zealous life. We are reminded that God watches over us. He sees into the depths of our hearts. We can fool people about our true selves. We can perform as required. We can gain approval from public authority. We can impress the mob. But God looks at the heart. Nothing fools Him.

Humility, then, is the mortal enemy of rebellion against God. To be subject to God we need to open our desires out into the light. St Benedict wants his monks to look within themselves – "the wish is the mother of the thought". To face the truth about what is going on within us is a key to avoiding negligence that begins and facilitates decline. This is a sober view of reality – St Benedict would have written with many years of experience, both of his own spiritual journey and that of being an abbot of a monastery. Such a view is the product of mature knowledge of the human condition seen in one's own life and witnessed in the lives of others.

The second and third steps of St Benedict can be run together under the title, "Doing God's Will". St Benedict sees that the second degree of humility is "that a person love not his own will nor take pleasure in satisfying his desires, but model his actions on the saying of the Lord, 'I have come not to do My own will, but the will of Him who sent Me'" (*John* 6:38). And the third degree of humility is that a person "for love of God submit himself to his Superior in all obedience". This call to obedience is a concept foreign to many today. We will explore the virtue of obedience in the next chapter. However, in the mind of St Benedict there cannot be growth in humility without a willingness to submit willingly to rightful authority.

Autonomy and freedom are considered to be found in the absence of restraint. Humility enables us to accept restraints. We are willing to accept that we are to live under direction or authority, both divine and human. The truth is that we cannot live free from restraints. The Christian realises that he must submit himself to Christ. We are not the sole determiners of our destiny.

The fourth step, following St Benedict, can be given the title "patience". St Benedict teaches, "The fourth degree of humility is that he hold fast to patience with a silent mind when in this obedience he meets with difficulties and contradictions and even any kind of injustice, enduring all without growing weary or running away".

Fr Casey comments that St Benedict is here proposing that virtue is found in accepting the discipline of others. Leadership may not always be competent, correct, or just. We may feel our gifts are not appreciated, our opportunities curtailed. The whole situation may seem stunting or at least frustrating. Here St Benedict proposes patience. St Benedict is speaking of obedience in irksome things, frustrating requirements. Obedience in things that don't bother us is no virtue. Patience means endurance in the right spirit. Not a grudging compliance, but a calm and tranquil spirit in the midst of frustration. Indeed, the test of being truly patient under trying situations is the degree of inner peace that is within us.

The fifth step for St Benedict is a challenging one. It refers to the particular system of monastic life and the role of the abbot in the community. We do need to adapt its recommendations to our situation. The call to a radical self honesty remains a key element in the maturing of the individual along the path to humility. St Benedict says, "The fifth degree of humility is that he hide from his abbot none of the evil thoughts that enter his heart or the sins committed in secret, but that he humbly confess them".

The key notion here is that if humility is truth, then the truth of ourselves needs to be brought out into the light. Deciding not to do this is to be open to delusion. Here it is not just the question of sacramental confession. It is the willingness to disclose our inner life to another. In this instance the other person is not just a peer who is sympathetic. St Benedict envisages the abbot. We can transpose this to being a spiritual director, a companion, a priest mentor, or some wise and holy guide. This is not so much a question of self-condemnation, where the other is a judge and executioner. Rather it is the disclosure that we may make to a doctor. "Yes, there is this pain and I need assistance to overcome it." The disclosure has to do with sins, with the inner darkness. It is not simply a safe disclosure of how we are faring in general. In order to do this we need to overcome our fear of intimacy, mistrust of authority, shame, self-sufficiency, or an unwillingness to be challenged.

The next three steps are taken together, for they all involve a common theme of self abasement. St Benedict says, "The sixth degree of humility is that a monk be content with the poorest and worst of everything." The seventh degree of humility is that "he consider himself lower and of less account than anyone else…" and the eighth degree is "that a monk do nothing except what is commended by the common Rule of the monastery and the example of the elders".

Abasement is a means of curbing our tendencies to domination, acquisition and social approval. A key question for us is whether we are subject to desires for self advancement, or possess a need for recognition or approval. Moving along this path of self abasement is necessary for anyone who wishes to grow in Christian character. It is something that can be addressed under good and healthy spiritual guidance.

The next three chapters of teaching by St Benedict also cover a common theme which can be summarised as restraint of speech. Again, quoting St Benedict, "The ninth degree of humility is that a monk restrain his tongue and keep silence, not speaking until he is questioned". The tenth degree of humility is "that he be not ready and quick to laugh" and the eleventh degree of humility is "that when a monk speaks he do so gently and without laughter, humbly and seriously, in few and sensible words, and that he be not noisy in his speech". We can see that this has particular application in a monastic setting. It seems an exotic concept for the contemporary world, full as it is with noise. Noise begets noise. As Christians we need to be able to enter into inner quiet. To become people of prayer we need to be able to hear the voice of God, and respond to the promptings of the Spirit. Silence leads to solitude. Solitude is the ground upon which the soul is able to breathe, and prayer is born.

Here is a call to foster an inner quiet by the disciplining of our speech. It is true that an excess of speech drains psychic energy. We do need to consider the dangers of excessive frivolity in speech. We need to challenge ourselves about our need for constant stimulation or activity because this can suggest a restlessness of spirit.

And so to the final step. It is proposed as a completion of the character of the monk: "The twelfth degree of humility is that a monk not only have humility in his heart but also by his very appearance make it always manifest to those who see him". St Benedict proposes here that the complete monk is not in some high mystical state, no exalted holiness, but rather he is one who is firmly wedded to the earth, his eyes cast down to the dust from whence he came. It is as though the humble person is thoroughly human, rather than gloriously other-worldly. But such a one is at once transparently human, serenely normal and yet an icon of God. The person does not get in the way of God. Something is perceived in the person that is of God, and it draws those who meet him to the mystery of God who is true and good and beautiful.

Such is the wisdom of St Benedict.

The foundation to a virtuous life

St Benedict saw the virtue of humility as the foundation upon which the monk could build a solid Christian character. We can also see that desiring humility is the way to grow in true Christian character. It is a foundation to growth in character but it is also the crown of a mature character. A person who has evidently grown in virtue and who is humble is an attractive and inspiring person. We quietly admire this quality. Somehow their greatness is all the more noble because it is clothed in humility.

There is a psalm that can be said with genuine desire that our own spirit will be humble before God and then before men.

> Yahweh, my heart is not haughty, I do not set my sights too high. I have taken no part in great affairs, in wonders beyond my scope. No, I hold myself in quiet and silence, like a little child in its mother's arms, like a little child, so I keep myself. (*Psalm* 131).

A Litany of Humility

Cardinal Merry del Val, Secretary of State to Pope St Pius X, used to recite this Litany of Humility after celebrating Mass each day. It is a worthy prayer for anyone wishing to grow in the virtue of humility.

O Jesus! meek and humble of heart: Hear me.

From the desire of being esteemed:

Deliver me, Jesus.

From the desire of being loved:

Deliver me, Jesus.

From the desire of being extolled:

Deliver me, Jesus.

From the desire of being honoured:

Deliver me, Jesus.

From the desire of being praised:

Deliver me, Jesus.

From the desire of being preferred to others:

Deliver me, Jesus.

From the desire of being consulted:

Deliver me, Jesus.

From the desire of being approved:

Deliver me, Jesus.

From the fear of being humiliated:

Deliver me, Jesus.

From the fear of being despised:

Deliver me, Jesus.

From the fear of suffering rebukes:

Deliver me, Jesus.

From the fear of being calumniated:

Deliver me, Jesus.

From the fear of being forgotten:

Deliver me, Jesus.

From the fear of being ridiculed:

Deliver me, Jesus.

From the fear of being wronged:

Deliver me, Jesus.

From the fear of being suspected:

Deliver me, Jesus.

That others may be loved more than I:

Jesus, grant me the grace to desire it.

That others may be esteemed more than I:

Jesus, grant me the grace to desire it.

That in the opinion of the world, others may increase, and I may decrease:

Jesus, grant me the grace to desire it.

That others may be chosen and I set aside:

Jesus, grant me the grace to desire it.

That others may be praised and I unnoticed:

Jesus, grant me the grace to desire it.

That others may be preferred to me in everything:

Jesus, grant me the grace to desire it.

That others become holier than I, provided that I may become as holy as I should:

Jesus, grant me the grace to desire it.

4.

The Freedom of Obedience

We noted that humility is an unfamiliar virtue to many today. So is the virtue of obedience. Though probably more than humility, obedience is a virtue strongly resisted by many. In an age of fierce individualism people presume the right to unfettered freedom. Like humility the virtue of obedience suffers from many misunderstandings. It, too, is seen as a denial of human self-determination. One of the particular issues that affects an understanding of obedience is the attitude towards authority. There is a lack of confidence in authority, which, at times, can become marred by cynicism.

This lack of confidence in authority has affected people's attitudes towards church teaching and leadership. Many are unprepared to accept Catholic teaching as a whole. They will question decisions of bishops and the Pope. They prefer to accept those elements with which they agree. There is an attitude of picking and choosing. This is what is sometimes referred to a person being a "Cafeteria Catholic". The issue at stake here is that people will accept only those things that make sense to them. They will obey those directions which accord with their own views. In other words, people have made themselves the authority.

We can speak of a crisis of authority in the Church and in the world today and with it a crisis of obedience.

What is obedience?

Obedience comes from a Latin word, *obedire*, which means to "to hearken to". Its base meaning carries with it the idea of listening.

Obedience is a freely chosen human act. It differs from compliance, which is the yielding to the demands of others, and differs from conformity, which is behavior intended to match that of the majority. Obedience is not about subjection to another - this is a denial of human dignity – but rather it is an expression of due recognition given to proper authority. To be truly a virtue it must be a freely chosen act. It can be defined as "The moral virtue that inclines the will to comply with the will of another who has the right to command."[74] The Catechism of the Catholic Church addresses the virtue of obedience, identifying it as a duty. "The duty of obedience requires all to give due honour to authority and to treat those who are charged to exercise it with respect, and, insofar as it is deserved, with gratitude and good-will."[75]

We need to consider the Christian understanding of the virtue of obedience, and to do this we will consider the obedience found in Jesus Christ.

Christ was "obedient unto death"

At the heart of the Christian mystery lies the virtue of obedience. The obedience of Christ was the subject of much reflection by the New Testament writers. For instance the *Letter to the Hebrews* speaks of Christ learning to obey through suffering.[76] It also refers to Christ as the obedient servant and Son who can say, "Here I am! I am coming to do your will".[77] The reason for this focus on the obedience of Christ is related to his obedience to the will of his Father in being prepared to

---

[74] Fr John Hardon, S.T.D. in his *Pocket Catholic Dictionary* (New York: Image Books, 1985), p. 291.

[75] *Catechism of the Catholic Church*, n. 1900.

[76] *Hebrews* 5:8.

[77] See *Hebrews* 10:9; cf *Hebrews* 10:7 where the author is quoting from *Psalm* 40:6-8, highlighting the fact that the sacrifice truly pleasing to God is that which is from the heart.

suffer death on the cross. This was obedience unto death.[78]

St Paul mentions the obedience of Christ many times and contrasts it with the disobedience of Adam. In *Romans*, chapter 5, he compares the disobedience of Adam bringing sin into the world and the obedience of Christ as the means of our redemption.

The obedience of Christ was in fact the foundation to his whole life and not just something realised through his acceptance of his crucifixion. Christ saw his whole life and mission as one of faithful obedience to the will of his Father. The Gospels reveal how this was a vital dimension of his life. He says that he lives to do the will of his Father: "My food is to do the will of the one who sent me, and to complete his work" (*John* 4:34). Similarly in *John* 5:30, Jesus says: "By myself I can do nothing. I can judge only as I am told to judge, and my judgment is just, because I seek to do not my own will but the will of him who sent me". The New Testament speaks of Jesus spending whole nights in prayer were a seeking of his Fathers' will.[79]

The Lord himself has a clear sense of the fact that his life is one of complete obedience to the will of his Father: "I have come from heaven, not to do my own will, but to do the will of him who sent me." (*John* 6:38). This comes into stark contrast in Gethsemane when Christ cries out, "*Abba*, Father! For you everything is possible. Take this cup away from me." Then, immediately, Jesus moves to his position of surrender to his Father's will, "But let it be as you, not I, would have it" (*Mark* 14:36). This is a poignant moment: the virtue of obedience

---

[78] See *Philippians* 2:6-11. St Paul emphasizes that we ought to have the same mind as that of Christ who humbled himself in obedience to his Father's will even to death.

[79] St Luke in particular emphasises this aspect of the life of Jesus. Thus, in 6:12, he notes, "Now it happened in those days that he went onto the mountain to pray; and he spent the whole night in prayer to God." St Luke particularly emphasises that the Lord withdrew to pray prior to making key decisions, like the naming of his disciples. This suggests that he sought the will of his Father prior to making key decisions.

rises above human fear. Obedience is a letting go of a desire to control our destiny and entrust it into the hands of God. The words of the Lord as he died express this: "Father, into your hands I commit my spirit" (*Luke* 23:46; *Psalm* 31:5).

Thus, we can see from this that the virtue of obedience is a virtue directly linked to the Gospel. This particular virtue, in a mysterious way, takes us to the heart of the salvific work of God in Christ. Obedience is the pathway for the redeeming action of Christ manifested on Calvary.

The virtue

Obedience is more than just a willingness to be co-operative. When fully embraced at the level of Christian virtue it becomes, as we have seen, a participation in the salvific work of God. Obedience, as we noted in the life of Christ, is connected to the will of God. A willingness to embrace an attitude of obedience opens one's life to the potential of the will of God being fully realised in our lives. We make ourselves more malleable in the hands of the master Potter.[80] The prophet Isaiah reminds us that God's ways are not our ways and his thoughts are high above our thoughts[81]. An obedient heart provides the context for God's purposes to be realised in ways that we could never have imagined. A spirit of obedience enables the plans and purposes of God being carried out in and through us. This can take our lives to heights of fruitfulness that we could never imagine.

The virtue of obedience is a pliability and responsiveness that is captured in what can be the prevailing disposition of our hearts: "Here I am, I come to do your will". There is no better model for us in this matter than the Blessed Virgin Mary who would respond to the Angel Gabriel, "I am the handmaid of the Lord, let what you have said

---

80 See *Jeremiah* 18:1-11

81 See *Isaiah* 55:8

be done to me". The liturgy of the Mass of the Annunciation carries this theme in the Second Reading from *Hebrews* 4:4-10 and in the Responsorial Psalm (*Psalm* 40) which has this phrase as the response.

The Will of God

In the Lord's Prayer we say, "Thy will be done", adding "on earth as in heaven". Each time we say this prayer we are asking that the will of God be "done" not only in heaven but on earth – in other words in my life. We ask that the will of God be fulfilled in me. For the Christian the desire of our hearts is to conform our lives to the will of God.

What is God's will for us? Scripture reveals an answer: "He wants everyone to be saved and reach full knowledge of the truth" (*1 Timothy* 2:4). We realise that God's action in our lives is ultimately for our own salvation. But this will of God works itself out in the particularity of our own individual lives. The eternal plan is expressed in concrete form in the lives of each individual Christian who is willing to open their lives to God.

God wants to act in and through us to achieve his purposes. On our part internal conformity and voluntary execution are our response. The will of God for us is not fate, or programmed inevitability. It is rather a call and an invitation. It is never a demand or a forced compliance.

To know and do the Will of God

How do we know the will of God? It is discovered internally. To make this discovery we must first be willing to listen with a desire to hear what God wants of us: "Speak, Yahweh, for your servant is listening" (*1 Samuel* 3:10). Our own hearts must be aligned to the will of God. What do you want of me? It cannot be a detached curious interest. To know the will of God one must be totally given over to it. The best example is the Blessed Virgin Mary. She could hear and respond because she was the "lowly handmaid".

In order for the will of God to be fulfilled in our lives we need to freed from a preoccupation with our own will and desires. This is not easy. This is the virtue – the decision I take to place my life in the hands of God. I freely choose to be led and directed by the will of God for me. St Paul puts this powerfully when he says, "I urge you, then, brothers, remembering the mercies of God, to offer your bodies as a living sacrifice, dedicated and acceptable to God; that is the kind of worship for you, as sensible people. Do not model your behaviour on the contemporary world, but let the renewing of your minds transform you, so that you may discern for yourselves what is the will of God – what is good and acceptable and mature" (*Romans* 12:1-2).

Obedience to authority

We have considered obedience thus far from the point of view of a Christian obedience to God. This is a personal and spiritual path. There are other dimensions to obedience that need to be considered. There is obedience to proper authority.

St Luke recounts that after being found in the temple Jesus returned to Nazareth with Mary and Joseph and "lived under their authority" (*Luke* 2:51). Jesus presents us with a model of obedience within the family. The home is where obedience is first learnt. The Fourth Commandment: "Honour your father and your mother, as Yahweh your God has commanded you, so that you may have long life and may prosper in the country which Yahweh your God is giving you"(*Deuteronomy* 5:16).

This commandment obliges children to honour their parents. However, the interpretation of it in the Old Testament and then in the New understood it to include respect and obedience to all legitimate authority. Children learning to honour their parents in a respectful obedience in the home will lay the foundation the more general respect for all rightful authority. The *Catechism of the Catholic Church* expresses it in this way, "The fourth commandment opens the second table of the Decalogue. It shows us the order of charity. God has willed that, after him, we should honour our parents to whom we owe life and who have handed on to us the knowledge of God. We are obliged to honour and respect all those whom God, for our good, has vested with his authority"[82].

The New Testament Scriptures urge Christians to be obedient to lawful authority. A pivotal passage is *Romans* 13:1-7. It is worth quoting in full.

> Everyone is to obey the governing authorities, because there is no authority except from God and so whatever authorities exist have been appointed by God. So anyone who disobeys an authority is rebelling against God's ordinance; and rebels must expect to receive the condemnation they deserve. Magistrates bring fear not to those who do good, but to those who do evil. So if you want to live with no fear of authority, live honestly and you will have its approval; it is there to serve God for you and for your good. But if you do wrong, then you may well be afraid; because it is not for nothing that the symbol of authority is the sword: it is there to serve God, too, as his avenger, to bring retribution to wrongdoers. You must be obedient, therefore, not only because of this retribution, but also for conscience's sake. And this is why you should pay taxes, too, because the authorities are all serving God as his agents, even while they are busily occupied with that particular task. Pay to each one what is due to each: taxes to the one to whom tax is due, tolls to the one to whom tolls are due, respect to the one to whom respect is due, honour to the one to whom honour is due.

Christ himself practised obedience to those in civil authority. His birth at Bethlehem was occasioned by a decree of the emperor ordering a census of all the people in the Roman Empire. When asked about respect for civil authority Jesus makes an important distinction. The story is a familiar one. Jesus is asked, "Is it permissible for us to pay taxes to Caesar or not?" He answers, "Show me a denarius.

---

[82] *Catechism of the Catholic Church*, n. 2197.

Whose portrait and title are on it?" "Caesar's," they said. He said to them, "Well then, pay Caesar what belongs to Caesar – and God what belongs to God" (*Luke* 20:21-25).

Christ's reply has become the foundation of the Church's teaching. Simply, the State has authority from God to govern its citizens in what concerns the temporal affairs of this life. Citizens, therefore, have the duty to obey civil authority. However, their obedience is conditional. The rights of God are not only primary, they are normative. Laws of the State and decrees of civil authority are binding in conscience only where and in so far as they conform to the laws of God. The Christian is meant to play a constructive role in the society which at times may require challenge and criticism of civil authority: "Their loyal collaboration includes the right, and at times the duty, to voice their just criticisms of that which seems harmful to the dignity of persons and to the good of the community"[83].

St Peter taught, "For the sake of the Lord, accept the authority of every human institution" (*1 Peter* 2:13). St Paul taught, as we quoted above, "Everyone is to obey the governing authorities" (*Romans* 13:1). Civil authority is to be obeyed, but this can be a particular issue when the religious rights of citizens are denied by the State authorities. "There are forms of government," the Second Vatican Council declared, "under which the public authorities strive to deter the citizens from professing their religion and make life particularly difficult and dangerous for religious bodies"[84]. The principle that guides Christians is what Peter said to the Sanhedrin: "Obedience to God comes before obedience to men" (*Acts* 5:29). The price for this statement has been in many cases in Christian history the ultimate witness of martyrdom.

However it is also important to point out that civil authority has certain duties and responsibilities. The *Catechism of the Catholic*

---

83 *Catechism of the Catholic Church*, n. 2238.
84 *Declaration on Religious Liberty*, 15.

Church teaches: "Those who exercise authority should do so as a service.... The exercise of authority is measured morally in terms of its divine origin, its reasonable nature and its specific object. No one can command or establish what is contrary to the dignity of persons and the natural law"[85]. The Catholic Catechism emphasises that political authorities are "obliged to respect the fundamental rights of the human person"[86]. Thus, the Catholic Catechism teaches that a citizen is not obliged to follow civil law when it is contrary to the demands of the moral order, to the fundamental rights of persons or the teachings of the Gospel.

The obedience of faith

St Paul, in the beginning of his *Letter to the Romans* speaks of the "obedience of faith" (*Romans* 1:5). It is an important coupling. The *Catechism of the Catholic Church* teaches: "By faith, man completely submits his intellect and his will to God. With his whole being man gives his assent to God the revealer. Sacred Scripture calls this human response to God, the author of revelation, "the obedience of faith."[87] Our obedience to the Church is an act of faith. The Council taught: "In forming their consciences, the faithful must pay careful attention to the sacred and certain teaching of the Church. For the Catholic Church is by the will of Christ the teacher of truth. It is her duty to proclaim and teach with authority the truth which is Christ and, at the same time, to declare and confirm by her authority the principles of the moral order which spring from human nature itself."[88]

Jesus told his disciples, "If you love me, you will keep my commandments" (*John* 14:15). Response to Jesus involves obedience to his teaching. The New Testament on a number of occasions urges

---

85 *Catechism of the Catholic Church*, n. 2235.
86 *Catechism of the Catholic Church*, n. 2237.
87 *Catechism of the Catholic Church*, n. 143.
88 *Dignitatis Humanaen*, n. 14.

the believers to be obedient to what they have been taught: St Paul congratulates them "for maintaining the traditions exactly as I passed them on to you" (*1 Corinthians* 11:2); "keep the traditions" (*2 Thessalonians* 2:15); "keep away from any of the brothers who lives an undisciplined life, not in accordance with the tradition you received from us" (*2 Thessalonians* 3:6); "keep as your pattern the sound teaching you have heard from me, in the faith and love that are in Christ Jesus. With the help of the Holy Spirit who dwells in us, look after that precious thing given in trust" (*2 Timothy* 1:13-14); "Pass on to reliable people what you have heard from me through many witnesses so that they in turn will be able to teach others" (*2 Timothy* 2:2).

The issue of obedience to Church teaching has been quite problematical in recent years. Particularly the response to *Humanae Vitae*[89] stirred up the question of whether a Catholic can dissent from Church teaching. In 1998, Pope John Paul II's motu proprio *Ad Tuendam Fidem* addressed the issue in these words, "Furthermore, each and everything set forth definitively by the Magisterium of the Church regarding teaching on faith and morals must be firmly

---

89 *Humanae vitae* was promulgated in July 1968. It stirred up strong reaction in many circles in the Church. Theologian Charles Curran composed a statement critical of the ecclesiology and methodology of the document. The statement concluded that "spouses may responsibly decide according to their conscience that artificial contraception in some circumstances is permissible and indeed necessary to preserve and foster the value and sacredness of marriage." This statement was eventually signed by over 600 theologians and other academics, including well-known theologians such as Bernard Haring, David Tracy, Richard McBrien, Walter Burghardt, Raymond Collins, Roland Murphy and Bernard McGinn. A group of European theologians met in Amsterdam on 18-19 September 1968 and issued a dissenting statement. The signatories included some of the best known theologians in Europe: J. M. Aubert, A. Auer, T. Beemer, F. Bockle, W. Bulst, P. Fransen, J. Groot, P. Huizing, L. Janssens, R. van Kessel, W. Klijn, F. Klostermann, E. McDonagh, C. Robert, P. Schoonenberg, M. de Wachter. The response issued in the notion of dissent from official Church teaching.

accepted and held; namely, those things required for the holy keeping and faithful exposition of the deposit of faith; therefore, anyone who rejects propositions which are to be held definitively sets himself against the teaching of the Catholic Church".[90] A Catholic seeks to have the attitude of "sentire cum Ecclesia", which is having a profound unity of spirit with the Church. *Psalm* 119 is a reflection on embracing the will and law of God. The psalmist says, "Your will is my delight; your statutes are my counsellors' (v. 24); Wonderful are your decrees; therefore I follow them (v. 29).

The Freedom of Obedience

Jesus taught, "You will come to know the truth, and the truth will set you free" (*John* 8:32). It is true that in the discovery of the truth about ourselves and the truth about human life we come to a new level of interior freedom. In a particular way, embracing the virtue of obedience is a path to inner freedom. The word we often hear today is the word "stress". Many people experience the stress of modern living. It is very true that modern life is stressful. But much of the stress people experience is an inner stress. It is the stress of trying to achieve, of trying to satisfying others. It is the stress of trying to construct the best possibilities for ourselves.

A person who is able to surrender their lives into the hands of God can discover being set free from stress. It is not that life's demands disappear, but we are more capable of living within these demands. Wanting to simply live each moment in union with God and under the grace of God can be a wonderfully freeing experience. We learn, for instance, to offer up the little frustrations of life to God, rather than see them as obstacles to our purposes. We have a sense that there is a greater plan and purpose to our existence than the trivial situations of the day-to-day. We open ourselves to the will of God as an overarching

---

[90] This teaching of Pope John Paul II sought to clarify the way in which Canon 750, §2 was to be understood.

and benevolent flow of grace in our lives. We learn trust and surrender and with these come peace and an inner calm.

We have been set free.

The Spiritual Doctrine of Jean-Pierre de Caussade

This Christian teaching on seeking and living the will of God is expressed beautifully in the spiritual teaching of Jean-Pierre de Caussade in his classic work, "Self-abandonment to Divine Providence". De Caussade was a Jesuit, living at the beginning of the 18th century. He was a Spiritual Director of nuns and the book was not his own work, but a production of the notes nuns took of his spiritual conferences. They offer a delightfully simple formula for growth in the Christian life. He teaches, "The presence of God which sanctifies our souls is that indwelling Holy Trinity which is established in the depths of our hearts when they submit to the divine will". In another place he counsels the nuns, "There is but one thing to do: to purify our hearts, to detach ourselves from creatures and to abandon ourselves entirely to God".

His simple teaching presents a great insight into the Christian life. A complete surrender in trust to God enables God's will to be the transforming element of our life. God can do in us even more than we can ever ask for or imagine.[91] A final statement of the theme of his spiritual teaching: "Faith is what I preach, self abandonment, confidence and faith: willingly to be the subject of divine action".

We can conclude this section looking at the virtue of obedience by Père de Caussade's "Prayer for the Blessed State of Self-Abandonment".

> O my God! When will it please thee to grant me the favour of living always in that union of my will with thy heavenly will? Where saying nothing all is said and all is done by leaving all to thee; where we achieve much by surrendering ever more to thy

---
91 See *Ephesians* 3:20.

will and yet are relieved of all toil since we place everything in thy care and are concerned only to trust wholly in thee. Blessed state, which, even in the absence of any conscious faith, offers the soul an inward and entirely spiritual disposition. So that, by the habitual inclination of my heart, I may constantly repeat: "Thy will be done!" Yes, my God, yes to whatever may please thee. May all thy holy wishes be fulfilled. I renounce mine which are blind, perverse and corrupted by that despicable ego, the mortal enemy of thy grace, thy perfect love, thy glory and my sanctification.

5.
Personal Integrity – Justice

If a person does not have the pursuit of virtue as a key element in their life, then decisions are often motivated by pragmatism. In other words a person will consider the usefulness of a decision, often apart from any consideration of its moral quality. A decision is made if it seems to meet certain needs and the outcome is one of benefit to the person. Pragmatism can also be understood as a pursuit of self-interest. A matter is assessed in terms of how it can be of personal benefit. Countries readily speak of "national self-interest". In other words decisions are made according to what is seen as in the best interests of the nation.

In democratic political life this often becomes the necessary "modus operandi" for the politician or political party. A politician is faced with the need to satisfy various conflicting interests, hence there is a pressure to surrender a principled stand for a pragmatic position that goes in part to satisfy the interested parties. This sort of pragmatism comes under the general notion of "utilitarianism".[92] Utilitarianism in a consumerist society finds expression in the pursuit of money and financial interests which prevail over ethical concerns. Utilitarianism is a theory which proposes that attaining the best possible consequences – that which provides the greatest good for the greatest number of persons – is considered the ethical course of action. Therefore, if we could save the lives of one hundred persons by killing

---

92 Utilitarianism is a philosophical approach which teaches that the end of human conduct is individual happiness. Thus the discriminating norm which distinguishes conduct into right and wrong is pleasure and pain. Its most distinguished advocate was the English philosopher, John Stuart Mill.

one individual then this is what we should do. In other words, the ends will justify the means.

Living as we do in a globalized world where there are people of different religions and cultures living side by side, such a pragmatic approach is often seen as the most practical way to operate on a day-to-day basis. We have an ethical pluralism which translates into moral relativism. It is the view of many today that there are no absolutes in the moral life since every culture has a different conception of what is good and right. Moral decisions are conditioned by a person's background, upbringing and culture. Many people today adopt the attitude that we cannot impose onto others our views of rightness and wrongness.

As we have mentioned before, individual freedom and the right to self-determination are understood as the greatest good and everyone should be given the choice to do what they like. This is in contrast to Catholic moral teaching which affirms the existence of a common human nature while present in cultural diversity. This common nature allows everyone to discover the law written within. The Catholic tradition speaks of the Natural Law.[93]

In the face of the pragmatism and moral relativism that we encounter every day, a Christian rightly asks: How can we develop patterns of right conduct whereby we are faithful to our understanding that there

---

[93] The *Catechism of the Catholic Church*, n. 1965, says of the Natural Law, "Man participates in the wisdom and goodness of the Creator who gives him mastery over his acts and the ability to govern himself with a view to the true and the good. The natural law expresses the original moral sense which enables man to discern by reason the good and the evil, the truth and the lie". It then quotes Pope Leo XIII, "The natural law is written and engraved in the soul of each and every man, because it is human reason ordaining him to do good and forbidding him to sin ... But this command of human reason would not have the force of law if it were not the voice and interpreter of a higher reason to which our spirit and our freedom must be submitted" (Leo XIII, *Libertas praestantissimum*, 597).

is a natural law governing all human beings and at the same time are able to live in a pluralistic society? In a way what we are seeking is a structure for personal integrity in a pluralistic world.

The Virtue of Justice

A way forward for us is to look at the virtue of Justice. This virtue is listed as one of the four Cardinal Virtues.[94] Today the notion of justice is often considered within the broader social context, rather than as a personal virtue. Within the Church there has been great attention given to questions of "Justice and Peace". Often this means that there is a focus on social justice rather than on the virtue of justice in one's individual life. A danger here is that justice can always been seen as "out there". It is someone else's issue. A person can adopt the higher moral ground, while not being aware of elements of justice to which they are blind. We see people today distressed at the killing of whales yet oblivious to the moral implications of abortion. Our enquiry will be centred on the question of developing the virtue of justice as a critical part of growing in full Christian character.

Plato in his book *Republic* identifies justice as the overarching virtue for individuals. For him almost every issue that he would regard as ethical comes under the notion of justice *(dikaosoune)*. The reason why Plato gives a prominent place to the idea of justice is that he was highly dissatisfied with the prevailing degenerating social and political conditions in Athens. He sought to describe the form of an ideal society in which justice reigned supreme. Plato's theory was that justice is

---

[94] There are four cardinal virtues: prudence, justice, temperance and fortitude. They are called cardinal (Latin: *cardo*, hinge) virtues because they are hinges on which all moral virtues depend. These are also called moral (Latin: *mores*, fixed values) because they govern our actions, order our passions, and guide our conduct according to faith and reason. The cardinal or moral virtues are natural, because they can be achieved through human effort, aided by grace.

a "human virtue" that makes a person self-consistent and good. On the social plane, justice takes the form of a social consciousness that makes a society internally harmonious and good.

Justice can be defined as the constant and perpetual will to render each person his due. The word "justice" comes from the Latin word *jus*, which means "right". St Thomas Aquinas in his *Summa Theologiae* teaches that the virtue of justice is founded upon the notion of *jus* (or right) because, according to the classical definition of the virtue, it is by justice that one renders to another his due by a perpetual constant will.[95] Justice, he teaches, directs man in his relations to others according to some kind of equality or rightness.[96] Justice, then, is based on the premise that each person has the right to receive his/her due, and the other has an obligation to render this due. A just person is one who habitually wills such a relation of equity.

St Thomas further explains that all human persons are equal in their rights, since their rights derive from their equal and common nature. He mentions that anything that does not share in the rational nature in which humans share, but has a non-rational nature has no rights of its own. Animals, strictly speaking, have no rights because they do not have dominion over their actions but are simply made to act. Thus we really cannot speak of "animal rights".

The *Catechism of the Catholic Church* describes the virtue of justice in these terms: "Justice is the moral virtue that consists in the constant and firm will to give their due to God and neighbour. Justice toward God is called the 'virtue of religion.' Justice toward men disposes one to respect the rights of each and to establish in human relationships the harmony that promotes equity with regard to persons and to the common good".[97]

---

95 *Summa Theologiae* II-II, 58, 1.
96 *Summa Theologiae* II-II, 57, 1; De Veritate 23, 6.
97 *Catechism of the Catholic Church*, n. 1807.

Justice, then, respects the rights of others, whether those rights are natural (right to life and freedom) or legal (contract rights, constitutional rights, civil rights). Should legal rights ever come into conflict with natural rights, however, the latter take precedence, and justice demands that they be respected first of all. Thus, law cannot take away the right of parents to educate their children. Nor can justice allow the granting of legal rights to one person (such as the "right to an abortion") at the expense of the natural rights of another (in that case, the infant in the womb). To do so is to fail "to give everyone his or her rightful due."

Justice as mutual debt

We hear people speak of a "debt of gratitude". What do they mean by that? Simply it means that persons sense that they are beholden to others because of what the others have contributed to them in some way. They have received something – it may be quite intangible – and they cannot simply pass without expressing appreciation for what they have received.

This universal human sense points to the fact that we are profoundly interrelated as human beings. We constantly receive from others. Justice is the virtue that touches upon this sense of debt we owe to others.

Justice then is the response we make to show appreciation for what we have received. It is deeply ingrained in the human spirit. One of the first ethical statements a child makes is "it's not fair". They have a sense of what is their due or what is the due to the other. Where there is an inequality they are quick to point it out. Human society functions when justice is done and is seen to be done.

Where justice is denied there grows a mounting sense of frustration and anger. It may be suppressed by harsh authority, but eventually it will burst forth. Harsh and brutal regimes will not last. Justice will have out in the end.

Thus we can say that a just person is first and foremost a grateful person. Where there is no gratitude there is no justice. An unjust person fails to see a relation of inequality between himself and another. He is blind. An unjust person is unable to recognize what has been given to him gratuitously. He operates under the general conviction that he is entitled to all he has received. He lacks a "debt of gratitude". A thoroughly unjust man has convinced himself of his superiority over others and everyone else is seen as a means to his personal ends.

The just man, on the other hand, recognizes his essential equality with every other human person. He does not believe he is somehow entitled to things. He is able to see when a specific behaviour has created a degree of inequality between himself and another. A just person has learned to be thoughtful. He naturally thinks of ways to make things "right" (jus).

We can note that there is a relationship between justice and humility. As we saw, humility is about truth. The humble man has made an accurate assessment of himself and has willingly accepted the truth of his status. He does not hope inordinately in himself.

The Just Man in the Scriptures

Scripture often speaks of the "just man". Many figures in the Old and New Testaments are given this title. The *Book of Job* for instance examines the question of suffering in the life of a just man. The first of the psalms describes the qualities of the just man. He has not followed the counsel of the wicked. He has not lingered among sinners. His will is united with the will of God. He meditates "day and night" on the law of God. Such a man is described as being like a tree planted near running waters – constantly refreshed he is able to continuously produce good fruit.

The notion of the just man is a topic in the Wisdom literature of the Old Testament. The *Book of Proverbs* proposes the worth of the just man over the sinful man. For the religious man the pursuit of justice is of paramount importance. Goodness has its own essential worth and will be the subject of reward from God.

In the New Testament, St Joseph is described as a just man. St John Chrysostom referring to St Matthew's comment that St Joseph was a just man said, "By 'a just man' [Matthew] means him who is virtuous in all things".[98] Applying the title "just" to a person recognises that this person is acceptable in the eyes of God and men. The just man is one who is faithful to his responsibilities, conducts his affairs with honour and can be trusted in all things. St Joseph was seen as such a man. Joseph was a man who faithfully and humbly carried out his duties and responsibilities. He sought nothing for himself but focussed his attention of what was expected of him. Pope John Paul II stated, "Recalling that God wished to entrust the beginnings of our redemption to the faithful care of St Joseph, [the Church] asks God to grant that she may faithfully cooperate in the work of salvation; that she may receive the same faithfulness and purity of heart that inspired Joseph in serving the Incarnate Word; and that she may walk before God in the ways of holiness and justice, following Joseph's example and through his intercession."[99]

Personal integrity

The goal of growth in the virtue of justice is to achieve personal integrity. Personal integrity assumes that a person has adhered to moral and ethical principles and has developed a soundness of moral character marked by honesty in all dealings with others. A person of integrity practices what he believes is right. Such a person considers principle rather than pragmatism. A "person of principle" not only understands the importance of principle in human dealings, but lives by principle. Truth, honesty, transparency are the marks of a person of

---

[98] Quoted by Thomas Aquinas, *Catena Aurea*, in *Matthew* 1:19.
[99] Pope John Paul II, *Redemptoris custos*, 31.

integrity. Such a person is not bowed by human pressures to conform, but stands firmly by the truth no matter what the cost.

For an individual to have personal integrity means that he has developed a harmony or integration between various elements of the self. A person of integrity is predictable and this engenders trust. Others can rely on such a person. To act without integrity, even occasionally, will leave others distrustful. Trust is built by consistent patterns of just behavior. Trust can be lost by one act of injustice or deceit.

Guarding the truth

The just person follows the Golden Rule – he will not do to others what he wills not to be done to himself.[100] Such a person is committed to speak the truth in all circumstances. To lie to another human person is to will a relationship of inequality. A person convinced of his essential superiority over others will readily lie, deceive, mislead, and manipulate. A person of integrity will always adhere to the truth. Lying leads to a person becoming someone who cannot be trusted. Thus, for the sake of some temporal benefit, a deficiency entered their character. The person given to lies has lost personal integrity. When one lies the truth is in the mind but not in the word. Hence a person is divided. Integrity is lost.

Lying can never be justified as a good action. Under normal circumstances, there is a moral responsibility to express ourselves truthfully to others in speaking and writing. If, for particular reasons, we have to withhold information from others (what is often called "mental reservation") we must not let this flow into telling a lie. To lie is to violate the requirement to treat others in a way that respects their status as persons equal in dignity to ourselves.

The virtue of justice in relation to faithfulness to the truth applies in commercial life. The Catholic Catechism teaches, "Promises must be kept and contracts strictly observed to the extent that the commitments

---

100 The golden rule: see *Tobit* 4:15; cf. *Matthew* 7:12; *Luke* 6:31.

made in them are morally just. A significant part of economic and social life depends on the honoring of contracts between physical or moral persons - commercial contracts of purchase or sale, rental or labor contracts. All contracts must be agreed to and executed in good faith."[101]

The common good

An individual player in a sports team understands that he is to work in conjunction with the other players to achieve the goal of victory in the contest. Victory is the common good of the team. The common good is essentially an immaterial but clearly discernible reality. Human beings live in a social environment and each is to contribute to the common good of the society. A just person will recognize that he is the beneficiary of the social whole, that is, of the labor of countless others before him. He will realize that what he possesses as common goods came about through the establishment of social conditions that preceded him, such as the existence of a free society, a just legal system, schools, universities, hospitals, and so on. Thus a just person wishes to return something to the society in appreciation of what he has received.

The civil community as a whole has an end and that end is the common good. The just person is motivated by gratitude to commit to this common good, to find ways to direct his labor towards the betterment of the civil community. The concerted effort of everyone to establish the common good enriches the lives of everyone within it.

The *Catechism of the Catholic Church* speaks of the common good in these terms, "The common good consists of three essential elements: respect for and promotion of the fundamental rights of the person; prosperity, or the development of the spiritual and temporal goods of society; the peace and security of the group and of its members."[102] We

---
101 *Catechism of the Catholic Church*, n. 2410.
102 *Catechism of the Catholic Church*, n. 1925.

note that persons always have priority over things; at the same time, particular interests of persons or of groups need to yield at times to the larger good of the community as a whole.

It teaches that in economic matters, "respect for human dignity requires the practice of the virtue of *temperance*, so as to moderate attachment to this world's goods; the practice of the virtue of *justice*, to preserve our neighbor's rights and render him what is his due; and the practice of *solidarity*, in accordance with the Golden Rule[103] and in keeping with the generosity of the Lord, who "though he was rich, yet for your sake ... became poor so that by his poverty, you might become rich."[104]

Stewardship and prodigality

The just person will exercise proper stewardship over what he possesses. Proper stewardship will be the mean between covetousness on the one hand, and prodigality on the other. A just person, as we have seen, recognizes the debt he owes to the civil community and so will use his excess wealth for good causes. He will be moved to respond to those who suffer and have less and contribute in creating conditions for their wellbeing. Almsgiving is a Christian virtue and is the mark of one who is just.

The Catholic Catechism teaches, "In his use of things man should regard the external goods he legitimately owns not merely as exclusive to himself but common to others also, in the sense that they can benefit others as well as himself. The ownership of any property makes its

---

[103] The Golden Rule or the ethic of reciprocity is found in the Scriptures. It is common to nearly every religion. It is often regarded as the most concise and general principle of ethics. It is a condensation in one principle of all longer lists of ordinances such as the Decalogue. It finds expression in the statement, "You will love your neighbour as yourself" (*Leviticus* 19:18) and "So always treat others as you would like them to treat you; that is the Law and the Prophets." (*Matthew* 7:12)

[104] *Catechism of the Catholic Church*, n. 2407.

holder a steward of Providence, with the task of making it fruitful and communicating its benefits to others, first of all his family."[105]

Prodigality is the opposite of proper stewardship. This is a vice by which a person is inclined to use his excess wealth for himself to gratify his passions. This can be accompanied by covetousness which is the inordinate love of possessing. Covetousness spawns a number of other vices against justice, such as fraud, lack of mercy, treachery, perjury, violence, and so on.

The virtue of justice also extends to the way in which we treat the natural environment. This issue has been at the forefront of discussion in society. The Church teaches, "The seventh commandment enjoins respect for the integrity of creation. Animals, like plants and inanimate beings, are by nature destined for the common good of past, present, and future humanity. Use of the mineral, vegetable, and animal resources of the universe cannot be divorced from respect for moral imperatives. Man's dominion over inanimate and other living beings granted by the Creator is not absolute; it is limited by concern for the quality of life of his neighbor, including generations to come; it requires a religious respect for the integrity of creation".[106]

Justice and forgiveness

Every time we say the Lord's Prayer, we say "forgive us our trespasses as we forgive those who trespass against us". The Gospels show that the Lord regarded forgiveness of others as a most important virtue. The parable of the Unjust Steward, found in *Luke* 16:1-8, highlights this virtue. The Lord compares the forgiveness of a considerable debt which the steward receives from his master (being forgiven by God) with his unwillingness to forgive his fellow servant who owes him a trifling amount. It is his fellow servants who are outraged by the blatant injustice and report it to the master.

---

[105] *Catechism of the Catholic Church*, n. 2404.
[106] *Catechism of the Catholic Church*, n. 2415.

How can justice and forgiveness be reconciled? It is natural to think that forgiveness nullifies justice. The administering of justice, we assume, is about punishment being applied to wrongdoing. This is retributive justice which restores things to their original state. This kind of justice has an important role to play in human society. However retributive justice cannot by itself create a truly just society. What this kind of justice can accomplish is always limited. It may deal with past events but it will not necessarily build the future. Forgiveness can dispense people from retributive justice in the cause of creating new possibilities for the future. In the end we can never fully "put things right". Forgiveness seeks not so much to right the past as to set people free to build the future.

In his 2002 World Day of Peace Message, Blessed John Paul II explored the interrelationship between justice and forgiveness. He had this to say:

> True peace therefore is the fruit of justice, that moral virtue and legal guarantee which ensures full respect for rights and responsibilities, and the just distribution of benefits and burdens. But because human justice is always fragile and imperfect, subject as it is to the limitations and egoism of individuals and groups, it must include and, as it were, be completed by the *forgiveness which heals and rebuilds troubled human relations from their foundations*. This is true in circumstances great and small, at the personal level or on a wider, even international scale. Forgiveness is in no way opposed to justice, as if to forgive meant to overlook the need to right the wrong done. It is rather the fullness of justice, leading to that tranquillity of order which is much more than a fragile and temporary cessation of hostilities, involving as it does the deepest healing of the wounds which fester in human hearts. Justice and forgiveness are both essential to such healing.[107]

The virtue of justice cannot be isolated from the virtue of forgiveness. While in a society their interrelationship can be quite

---
107 Pope John Paul II, *World Day of Peace Message*, 1 January 2002, n. 3.

complex, both virtues need each other. In recent times "Truth and Reconciliation Commissions"[108] have come to have a vital place in redressing grave violations of personal rights imposed by repressive regimes, like South Africa under apartheid. For the future good of the society simply handing out retributive justice for serious crimes has been seen as not enough. These processes recognized the place of restorative justice[109] which has come to have a greater role in societies wishing to rebuild the social fabric after a period of grave injustices.

The just person is prudent

In exploring the virtue of justice we can add two other companion virtues which contribute to the achievement of personal integrity.

One who strives for personal integrity will hold the virtue of justice in high regard. Not only would such a person strive to ensure that justice was done, but would be vigilant in their own life to ensure that all their actions were marked by justice and truth. The cultivation of personal integrity will mean that a person has a profound respect for the other and wants all their actions to be measured and fair. A companion virtue that assists in this is the virtue of prudence.

Aristotle defined prudence as *recta ratio agibilium*, "right reason applied to practice." Prudence involves distinguishing between what is right and what is wrong. It is the ability to look at a concrete situation and know what ought to be done. It is the ability to make

---

108 The Truth and Reconciliation Commission in South Africa was a court-like process which sought restorative justice. Witnesses who were victims of serious human rights violations were invited to give statements about their experiences in public hearings. Those who were the perpetrators of violence could also give testimony and request amnesty from both civil and criminal prosecution.

109 Restorative justice is now used in the criminal justice system and emphasizes repairing the harm caused by unjust or criminal behaviour. It seeks to enable the parties themselves meet cooperatively to decide how to do this. This can lead to transformation of people, relationships and communities.

right judgments. Prudence gives us the knowledge of what must be done, when it must be done, and how it must be done.

Prudence is sometimes called "the mother of the virtues" because by it a person recognizes their moral duty and the good means by which to accomplish it. Prudence, then, is tied to the meaning of goodness. A person who is prudent will seek to accomplish the good. No other virtue can contradict what is prudent. Therefore, what is prudent is substantially what is good, and prudence is the measure of the other cardinal virtues – justice, temperance and fortitude.

The just person is wise

Along with being prudent, the just person will exhibit wisdom. This virtue is important as the practical way in which a person acts with integrity. Wisdom is acquired over time. It is the fruit of a life of acting with integrity.

There is a body of writings in the Old Testament which are called the Wisdom Literature. It includes the Psalms, the Book of Job, along with Proverbs, Ecclesiastes, the Song of Songs and the Book of Wisdom. These books offer the practical science of life inspired by Divine Revelation. It was often couched in proverbs and parables. They took their orientation from the divine Law as presented in Sacred Scripture and offered insight into how a person can lead a moral life.

The Wisdom literature reflects the spiritual and moral tradition of Israel and is based in the observation of the living human life. Wisdom is to be garnered from experience both personal and corporate. The way of wisdom is grounded in social structures and proven ways of doing things. At its heart is a deep reverence for God. It is God who has embedded truth in all of creation. Creation reflects the wisdom, nature, and character of its Creator, and therefore all of creation is a way to learn about God and his purposes for the world.

Human responsibility to God involves finding God's truth in the world, as reflected in its operations according to its creator's harmony, and then living within that harmony. Being wise is to search for and maintain the order of God in the world in order to live well as God has created humanity to live; a "fool"[110] is one who does not recognize God as creator and therefore does not seek to live according to the harmony of God's creation.

The "way of wisdom" is an ethical system in which humanity is responsible for searching, finding, and doing the things necessary to secure their well being in God's world.

Becoming a just person

As we have noted, the environment in which we live and work can raise many challenges to the practice of justice and to developing personal integrity. Often it will require great courage to stand for integrity. The Christian will encounter the culture of an organization to which he belongs – his place of employment, social clubs – that are not committed to the ideals of justice and integrity. Pragmatism and utilitarianism can cause a crisis of conscience for the Christian. At times a person may have to jeopardize their job for the sake of standing for truth and integrity. Such a decision is made because the person realises that this virtue is vital to forming true Christian character. At times a Christian may have to pay a heavy price for the acquisition of this virtue. In such situations he may cry out for divine justice to somehow right the wrong being perpetrated, but in the short term will have to accept the cost of standing for integrity.

The Psalms on a number of occasions present the prayer of the just man in the face of challenges in preserving his integrity. These psalms can be very appropriate prayers for one who seeks to grow in personal integrity. The following is taken from *Psalm* 26[111]:

---

110 In the Scriptural world the word "fool" is used as the designation of a person who is the opposite to being wise. It is commonly used, for instance, in the *Book of Proverbs*. "The fear of Yahweh is the beginning of knowledge; fools spurn wisdom and discipline" (*Proverbs* 1:7).
111 The translation used is that of the Grail version. This is the version used in the Divine Office.

Give judgment for me, O Lord,
for I have walked in my integrity.
I have trusted in the Lord; I have not wavered.

Examine me, Lord, and try me.
O test my heart and my mind.
Your mercy is before my eyes,
and I walk according to your truth.

I never take my seat with liars,
and with hypocrites I shall not go.
I hate the evildoer's company;
I will not take my seat with the wicked.

I wash my hands in innocence
and take my place around your altar,
singing a song of thanksgiving,
recounting all your wonders.
O Lord, I love the house where you dwell,
the place where your glory abides.

Do not sweep away my soul with sinners,
nor my life with those who shed blood,
in whose hands are evil plots,
whose right hands are filled with a bribe.

As for me, I have walked in my integrity.
Redeem me and have mercy on me.
My foot stands on level ground:
I will bless the Lord in the assembly.

6.
Chastity – the Guardian of Love

In choosing to live a virtuous life, one issue that is an area of intense struggle is that of sexual desire. The virtue involved here is chastity. The prevailing attitudes in our society give little if any support to the Christian striving to live out the virtue of chastity. In fact we live in an environment that daily challenges the practice of this virtue. It is the virtue that many find a constant struggle. Whether it be the barrage of sexually explicit images or a question often asked in sincerity is – "If two people love each other, shouldn't they be able to express their love through sexual intercourse?" There are constant messages proposing the opposite view – sex is to be enjoyed.

There are so many subtle arguments mounted against the virtue of chastity, particularly in the popular media. We are constantly confronted by films or TV sitcoms which portray romantic relationships that become sexually expressed. Our emotions are enticed to approve this expression of love. How often is chastity held up as a moral ideal? In fact chastity is seen by many as an obstacle to love. It is seen as denying what is most human and natural.

The question of chastity has been a particular point of strong contrast between the Christian understanding of life and the accepted attitudes of contemporary society. Often the traditional teaching of the Church is seen as out of touch with reality. It is also the case that many view the Church as having a set of rules which it seeks to impose on people's lives.

A personalist approach

The Church often receives criticism about its teaching on sexuality. It is often depicted as laying down unreasonable laws. Yet the question is: what is the true meaning of human sexuality and what is the path to true happiness in relationships? Blessed John Paul II has made a great contribution to meeting these criticisms by his personalist approach to marriage and sexuality. His starting point is the human person, rather than theoretical teaching on the subject. Particularly through the series of Wednesday audiences which now have become popularly known as the "Theology of the Body" he has presented the traditional Catholic teaching in a form and language that is accessible to this generation.[112] "Theology of the Body" has become a very popular subject among many young people wishing to live chaste lives. It has provided them with a clear rationale for their pursuit of this virtue and enabled them to defend their position amongst their contemporaries.

We will approach the question of the virtue of chastity from this personalist aspect.

Romantic love is associated primarily with the emotions or the sexual pleasure we receive from the person of the other sex. We tend to think of love only in its subjective aspect. The subjective aspect of love is the psychological experience—something which we experience interiorly. When men and women encounter each other, they may spontaneously find themselves physically attracted to the other. These natural sensual desires and emotional responses are not bad. In fact, they can serve as the "raw material" from which authentic love might develop. However, these responses do not represent love itself. At this level, they remain attractions to the other and are not true love for the other person in themselves.

The true nature of human love is much more than a psychological

---

[112] Theology of the Body is the topic of a series of 129 lectures given by Pope John Paul II during his Wednesday audiences between September 1979 and November 1984.

experience. It considers what is really happening in the relationship. True human love involves a decision of the will to want what is best for the other person, and the desire to want to see the person achieve what is best for them. This love involves a self-giving—a surrendering of one's will, a decision to limit one's autonomy in order to serve the other more freely.

Thus for a person in a close relationship with someone the question is not whether I have strong feelings and desire for the other, but rather whether the relationship has the maturity and commitment to make self-giving love possible. Ultimately such a maturity will mean that the relationship is made final and complete in the marriage covenant.

Chastity: the guardian of love

Before entering marriage a person will have a range of experiences of meeting different people to whom he/she is attracted. Indeed, after marriage this reality does not cease. It is important to examine a little more closely the nature of such relationships.

The experience of sensual desire or emotional longing for a person of the opposite sex whom we have met is a natural tendency. Such reactions can happen in an instant. Indeed such sensual and emotional responses can be so powerful that they dominate how we view the other person. Because of our fallen human nature, we can tend to see persons of the opposite sex primarily through the prism of their sexual attractiveness. This obscures our capacity to see them as persons. The person thus becomes a means for the meeting of our own needs. There is an egoism here. The precise value of the virtue of chastity is that it provides the orientation to approaching the other in such a way that we can integrate our sensual and sentimental attractions with authentic love for the other as a person. This virtue protects the true nature of our relationships with those of the opposite sex. In fact we can see that the virtue of chastity is necessary in order for us to be able to truly love. Far from something that hinders our love, chastity is what makes love possible. It protects love from falling into selfish, utilitarian attitudes and enables us to love selflessly.

The chaste man and the chaste woman become capable of true love.

Redeeming eros

Pope Benedict has built upon the teaching of Pope John Paul II in his first encyclical, "God is love."[113] In a bold assault on the views of contemporary society Pope Benedict sought to claim back the true notion of eros, from its current debasement as the erotic, the pornographic, to being what it is really is as the beauty of natural sexual love. He says of eros (natural sexual love):

> Nowadays Christianity of the past is often criticized as having been opposed to the body; and it is quite true that tendencies of this sort have always existed. Yet the contemporary way of exalting the body is deceptive. *Eros*, reduced to pure "sex", has become a commodity, a mere "thing" to be bought and sold, or rather, man himself becomes a commodity. This is hardly man's great "yes" to the body. On the contrary, he now considers his body and his sexuality as the purely material part of himself, to be used and exploited at will. Nor does he see it as an arena for the exercise of his freedom, but as a mere object that he attempts, as he pleases, to make both enjoyable and harmless. Here we are actually dealing with a debasement of the human body: no longer is it integrated into our overall existential freedom; no longer is it a vital expression of our whole being, but it is more or less relegated to the purely biological sphere. The apparent exaltation of the body can quickly turn into a hatred of bodiliness. Christian faith, on the other hand, has always considered man a unity in duality, a reality in which spirit and matter compenetrate, and in which each is brought to a new nobility. True, *eros* tends to rise "in ecstasy" towards the Divine, to lead us beyond ourselves; yet for this very reason it calls for a path of ascent, renunciation, purification and healing.

---

113 Its Latin title is *Deus caritas est* and it was the first encyclical letter of Pope Benedict XVI, given on 25 December 2005.

This is a beautiful and powerful testament to the fact that Christianity does not deny the natural aspect of sexuality, but actually is the way in which it can be brought to its true expression.

Eros so easily can be debased into what we call "lust". This lust is disordered sexual desire. Under the influence of sin, man is constantly tempted to desire the other as an object for his own pleasure, in other words, to use the other for his own satisfaction. Blessed John Paul II in his "theology of the body" talks stated:

> The body is not subordinated to the spirit as in the state of original innocence ... Lust, and in particular the lust of the body, is a specific threat to the structure of self-control and self-mastery, through which the human person is formed ... For the man, shame united with lust will become an impulse to 'dominate' the woman ... From the moment when the man 'dominates' her, the communion of persons – made of the full spiritual union of the two subjects giving themselves to each other – is followed by a different mutual relationship. This is the relationship of possession of the other as the object of one's own desire.[114]

Lust is eros turned into the selfish pursuit of personal satisfaction. But eros, as Pope Benedict teaches, can be redeemed. It is redeemed as the Pope teaches when it is "compenetrated" with the spiritual. Eros, in fact, can lead us beyond ourselves in the quest for the Divine.

A note about celibacy for the Kingdom of Heaven

In considering how eros can be redeemed we should speak a little about the question of celibacy, celibacy for the sake of the Kingdom of Heaven. If there is one thing that confounds modern society it is the choice that a young man or woman makes to live celibate for the sake of the Kingdom of God. The Lord himself knew that this decision would be a challenge to people. "It is not everyone who can accept what I have said, but only those to whom it is granted. There are

---

114 See Wednesday audience, 28 May 1980.

eunuchs born so from their mother's womb, there are eunuchs made so by human agency and there are eunuchs who have made themselves so for the sake of the kingdom of Heaven. Let anyone accept this who can" (*Matthew* 19:11-12). It is clear from our reading of the *Book of Genesis* that marriage is the natural path for human life. So someone who decides not to marry – not because they do not want to but because they are prepared to sacrifice their natural desire for the sake of God's call – seems to be going against nature. There is still a nuptial concept here. Some are called to be the spouse of Christ (women religious) or the spouse of the Church (priests and male religious) and live a celibate life for the sake of the Kingdom of Heaven. Men and women who live this commitment are a sign that we are all made for union with God, which is the ultimate fulfilment of the human person.

Blessed John Paul teaches, "Continence for the kingdom of heaven…is a charismatic sign. The human being…who, in the earthly situation where people usually marry, freely chooses continence for the sake of the kingdom of heaven, indicates that in that kingdom, which is the other world of the resurrection, people will no longer marry. This is because God will be 'everything to everyone.' In him [the risen man] there will be revealed, I would say, the absolute and eternal nuptial meaning of the body in union with God himself through the 'face to face' vision of him…"[115] He comments that "Conjugal love which finds its expression in continence for the kingdom of heaven must lead in its normal development to paternity or maternity in a spiritual sense."[116]

Eros is transformed to the spiritual plane when celibacy is chosen for the sake of God's Kingdom. Celibacy has both a nuptial meaning on the spiritual level, and it gives rise to spiritual paternity and maternity. Nature is not twisted by celibacy but simply transformed to another plane.

---

115 Wednesday audiences, 24 March 1982.
116 Wednesday audiences, 14 April 1982.

Contemporary Challenges to Masculine and Feminine identity

Another contemporary issue that bears in on our understanding of chastity in relationships is that of masculine and feminine identity. Chastity is best served when there is a clear understanding of the nature of being a man or a woman. Chastity flourishes in relationships which enhance the true character of the masculine and the feminine.

Today society throws up the challenges to the nature of masculinity and femininity. We are living in a period of history when the traditions in regard to identity of men and women is being challenged and changed.

I do not need to catalogue all the changes that are occurring, but to mention a few:

- The feminist movement has sought to restructure the place and role of women in society. We have witnessed very significant changes in the way women view themselves and their place in society. Some of this has been good. Some has been detrimental.
- The growing use of the word "gender" rather than "masculinity" or "femininity" has also caused some issues. The notion of gender proposes that a person can construct their sexual identity. Can sexual differences be so reduced that a person can construct an identity which is neither masculine nor feminine?
- The strong homosexual lobby seeks to redefine the nature of sexual relationships. Their arguments have swayed many. Society is moving to accept same sex relationships as being a normal alternative.
- There is a move to redefine marriage. Many argue that it cannot be restricted to a covenanted relationship between a man and a woman established for life.

Blessed John Paul II was aware of the dramatic changes that were occurring in society. He identified, as he said in *Evangelium vitae*, that the "eclipse of a sense of God" will lead to an "eclipse of man".[117] In

---

117 See *Evangelium vitae*, n. 21.

other words as modern man loses a sense of God, so his understanding of the nature of human life will be lost.

We need also to recognise that the new influences in society have strong backers. The United Nations organisations have been active in trying to bring about cultural change under the premise of "rights of women". Governments are being induced to change their policies in a range of areas that affect marriage and family life. There is a serious effort being waged to actually change the culture. There is an effort to bring in global ethical norms which reflect a deconstructed notion of the human person. Thus, the question of having a true understanding of our identity as men and women is of vital importance. We must begin by developing a clearer understanding of the forces that are at work around us.

"Individual" and "Person"

One of the questions we need to investigate is the emphasis on the "individual", rather than the "person". When we speak of the individual we cease to offer clear identity, as also when we speak of "partners" rather than spouses, or husband and wife. The use of the term is actually an objectification of human beings. When we use the notion of individual we immediately move to speak of "rights". It is the defining of someone in terms of themselves as against others. The notion of the individual easily moves to self-interest. The individual will tend to define themselves in terms of their own needs and desires. Thus we see a focus on self-fulfilment – I must be able to realise myself. This so easily becomes selfish, a narcissism. When the human being is viewed as an individual all relationships become matters of negotiation. There is a trade taking place, with the underlying attitude, "what is in it for me?"

A person, on the contrary, is someone who possesses a dignity and identity as a unique being. The use of the term person proposes the idea of relationships. A person is seen not so much in terms of rights, but in terms of relationships and hence there is a focus on the other, the recognition of the other. The person is one who is open to giving. Ultimately the notion of person has to do with love.

The efforts to change our way of speaking about human relationships promotes a change in the way we perceive our relationships. Language is a powerful tool that is being used to change our way of thinking, our way of seeing things. There is a process here of deconstructing the past so that a new future can be built. This future proposes a new way of seeing human beings. It is a future without reliance on the insights and wisdom of the Christian faith.

Sexual identity

The challenge today is to appreciate the true nature of sexual identity. In other words, what it means to be a woman and a man. Sexual identity belongs not just to the body, but to the person. The pursuit of equality between men and women in relationships and in society does not require surrender of sexual identity, but rather it is precisely through sexual identity that we discover our true self. Contrary to the feminist view, true self fulfilment is not denied if one seeks to be fully man or woman. Indeed the human person, being realised in two modalities needs the full expression of each to ensure that humanity is properly realised. Society is incomplete if masculinity or femininity are not appropriately realised respectively in each person.

The key to this as we saw earlier is the complementary nature of man and woman. Human nature is realised in two expressions which are meant to complete each other, and not to be in some sort of competition with each other. Indeed, men need women to be fully women (that is, embracing their femininity to the full) in order to complement their masculinity, and vice versa. Society is built on the ways in which men and women contribute to each other from their masculinity or femininity.

These changes in understanding have serious implications for the way in which society views the nature of marriage.

Husband and wife

Marriage is the primary institution in society. It is often said that a society is as strong as its marriages and family life. The Church has long understood this and has been active in promoting marriage and family life. Of the many challenges to a correct understanding of marriage in contemporary society, one that deserves attention, is that of the nature of the relationship between a man and a woman in marriage.

As we have been discussing the question of identity, it is important that we see it in terms of the roles embraced in marriage. A person's identity as man or woman is clarified through the experience of marriage. A couple discovers the character of complementarity more acutely. We cannot truly understand masculinity and femininity without being aware of its expression in marriage and family. The *Book of Genesis*, as we saw, immediately mentions that a man leaves his parents and joins himself to his wife and they become one. Human beings are meant for marriage. They find their full identity in marriage

Let us consider first the nature of being a husband and wife. In the marriage ceremony the couple are asked three questions by the celebrant. The first question is: Have you come here freely and without reservation to give yourselves to each other in marriage? It may seem a perfectly obvious question which does not have to be asked. Certainly in the modern period when marriages are in the main the result of a couple meeting and falling in love, couples approach the altar expressing a free and personal desire to marry. The question does highlight however not just that marriage is something freely chosen, but that the couple are willing "to give themselves to each other in marriage". Marriage is a giving of oneself. What is important is the giving and not the receiving. Certainly one receives, but the motivation for marriage is the desire to give.

A man then can see the first meaning in being a husband. It is to freely give himself to his wife. St Paul teaches men about marriage in these words, "Husbands should love their wives, just as Christ loved the Church and sacrificed himself for her to make her holy by washing her in cleansing water with a form of words, so that when he took the Church to himself she would be glorious, with no speck or wrinkle or anything like that, but holy and faultless. In the same way, husbands must love their wives as they love their own bodies; for a man to love his wife is for him to love himself. A man never hates his own body, but he feeds it and looks after it; and that is the way Christ treats the Church, because we are parts of his Body" (*Ephesians* 5:25-30).

St Paul sets the standard for men as being that of Christ's love for the Church. We can draw out three elements in the nature of Christ's love for the Church and see this as typifying the nature of the love of a husband for his wife. The love of Christ is unconditional. He knew the sinful state of humanity. He knew infidelity of humanity. He knew that humanity would fail to truly love Him in return. Yet Christ loved completely. Secondly, his love is a humble love. He is God, yet he became as we are. He laid aside his prerogatives as God (see *Philippians* 2:5-11). Jesus forgot himself and his own "rights", and rather centred on our needs. Thirdly, Christ loved sacrificially. He was prepared to lay down His life, dying for love of us.

Thus a Christian husband loves his wife unconditionally, humbly and sacrificially. His love is unconditional because it is a love is not based on external appearances, or the wife's capacity to organise the home, or give her attention to the husband's needs. It is a love based on the example of Christ. A Christian husband will not be concerned about his status in the family. He will listen to his wife, value her opinion, work closely with her in taking care of the children and the home. He will offer a humble service. A Christian husband is prepared in the end to lay down his life in the sense that he gives of himself without counting the cost.

A similar line could be explored for the love of a woman for her husband. This presentation in Scripture sets the tone for the nature of the love between husband and wife.

The second question asks: will you love and honour each other for the rest of your lives? This question reminds the couple that the nature of their union – which is a permanent union – is one of love and honour for each other. The question asked is not: *do* you love and honour each other? But *will* you love and honour each other? This reminds us that love is an act of the will. It is a choice that is made. It is, by definition, a self sacrificing love. It is love which is not just emotion but is a decision.

The third question that the couple are asked is: will you accept children lovingly from God and bring them up according to the law of Christ and his Church? This third question reminds the couple that their commitment to each other in marriage is really only completed when they have a child. Marriage is oriented towards family. Children are not an optional extra but are integral to the meaning of the marriage commitment. Very simply, as the biology of sexuality shows, love gives life. The act of conjugal love is intended to give life. Indeed, a couple can say that their married love is made complete when they conceive a child.

This introduces the couple to the new and completed aspect to their sexual identity – fatherhood and motherhood. Fatherhood and motherhood is more than biological generation. They are certainly more than a social or symbolic function. The child born from the intimate act of love between a husband and wife needs both father and mother. Each contributes to the child from the characteristics of their masculinity and femininity.

The companion virtue of modesty

The virtue of chastity is the guardian of love and the virtue of modesty is the companion virtue to assist in developing chastity. Modesty is an attitude of propriety and decency in dress, grooming, language, and behaviour. If we are modest, we do not draw undue attention to ourselves. St Paul says in his *First Letter to Timothy*, "Similarly, women are to wear suitable clothes and to be dressed quietly and modestly, without braided hair or gold and jewellery or expensive clothes; their adornment is to do the good works that are proper for women who claim to be religious"(*1 Timothy* 2:9-10). In his *Letter to the Corinthians*, St Paul says, "you have been bought at a price. So use your body for the glory of God" (*1 Corinthians* 6:20). It is the inward beauty that is important.

In his *First Letter to Timothy* referred to above, St Paul speaks of modesty in dress. The Greek word for "modesty" is *kosmios* which means "orderly, well-arranged, decent". *Kosmios* is from *kosmos* which refers to the "order" God established before the Original Sin.

Modesty aims to conform the exterior of a person – clothing, way of talking, bearing – to the interior sense of our dignity as sons and daughters of God. The shame of immodesty is directly connected with the Fall. Adam and Eve were naked before the Fall and felt no shame. After the Fall they covered themselves in an attempt to recover the dignity that they had lost. Only in marriage, where the spouse is a total gift – body and soul – to the other, is there no shame in revealing the vulnerability of our incompleteness.

Things that are considered holy are veiled, for example, the tabernacle in a church. Thus we veil our bodies as a sign of their sacredness. Contemporary culture tells us that our bodies are commodities to be displayed. There is a pre-occupation with "body image" in contemporary culture. This particularly affects women. Magazines constantly propose how we should look. There is an enormous pressure particularly on young women to conform to expectations in this area. This attitude to the body is in fact a dualism because it sees our bodies as something apart from who we are. Nevertheless, there are great pressures coming from our society.

The way we dress communicates a great deal about our self-understanding. The way we dress is simply a part of how we communicate to the world. Fashions today often tend to be about putting out a message. The question we need to ask ourselves is: what message am I communicating in the way I dress? Fashions do declare certain attitudes to life. One has only to look at what is being broadcast on tee-shirts these days. Glossy magazines through their pictures of men and women are portraying images of attitudes to life. They are presented attractively and seductively. It is hard not to desire to be like these images.

While the issue of modesty rests equally with men and women it is women who are most affected by this issue. Men and women are different in the ways in which they approach the opposite sex. Women are drawn to a quality of relationship while men are more visual in engaging with women. A woman's body language influences how a man will respond to her. If a woman dresses with dignity and carries herself with grace most men will approach that woman with respect and honour. On the other hand, if a woman dresses immodestly a man can be drawn to see her simply as a sexual object.[118]

This does not mean that women should dress in boring or unattractive ways. There is a way of dressing that does bring out the naturalness and beauty of true God-given femininity and masculinity.

---

[118] The issue of the sexualisation of both women and men has been the subject of strong critique by women writers. For example, Melinda Tankard Reist, who describes herself as a feminist, has been every active in arguing that pervasive and extreme pornographic depiction of women's sexual expression has a degrading and negative influence on both young women and men's sexuality. She has written extensively on the effects on the porn industry on the young. She has campaigned vigorously against the inappropriate sexualisation of children in advertising and marketing.

Women can reclaim the dignity and beauty of femininity. Men, too, in their forms of dress can radiate the true nature of masculinity.

Mention should also be made of modesty in relation to speech. Here we are concerned with what are called "impure jokes". Humour of its nature is good. A healthy character is one capable of seeing the funny side of life and being able to laugh. However the Scriptures warn about inappropriate subjects for speech. "There must be no foul or salacious talk or coarse jokes – all this is wrong for you; there should rather be thanksgiving" (*Ephesians* 5:4). Earlier in his *Letter to the Ephesians*, St Paul teaches, "No foul word should ever cross your lips; let your words be for the improvement of others, as occasion offers, and do good to your listeners" (*Ephesians* 4:29). Similarly, one reads in his *Letter to the Colossians*, "but now you must also must give up all these things: human anger, hot temper, malice, abusive language and dirty talk" (*Colossians* 3:8).

Resisting telling impure jokes is one thing and not too difficult to achieve, knowing how to respond in situations where such jokes are told is another. When we show our disapproval we are quickly dubbed a prude or something similar. We are told to "lighten up". This is the price we pay for seeking purity of mind and heart.

Another companion virtue – custody of the eyes

St Francis of Assisi encouraged his brother friars to foster custody of the eyes. He used a parable of a King's two messengers to show how the custody of the eyes protects the virtue of chastity.

> A certain pious King sent two messengers successively to the Queen with a communication from himself. The first messenger returned and brought an answer from the Queen, which he delivered exactly. But of the Queen herself he said nothing because he had always kept his eyes modestly cast down and had not raised them to look at her. The second messenger also returned. But after delivering in a few words the answer of the

Queen, he began to speak warmly of her beauty. "Truly, my lord," he said, "the Queen is the most fair and lovely woman I have ever seen, and thou art indeed happy and blessed to have her for thy spouse." At this the King was angry and said: "Wicked servant, how did you dare to cast your eyes upon my royal spouse? I believe that you may covet what you have so curiously gazed upon." Then he commanded the other messenger to be recalled, and said to him: "What do you think of the Queen?" He replied, "She listened very willingly and humbly to the message of the King and replied most prudently." But the Monarch again asked him, "But what do you think of her countenance? Did she not seem to you very fair and beautiful, more so than any other woman?" The servant replied, "My lord, I know nothing of the Queen's beauty. Whether she be fair or not, it is for thee alone to know and judge. My duty was only to convey thy message to her." The King rejoined, "You have answered well and wisely. You who have such chaste and modest eyes shall be my chamberlain. From the purity of your eyes I see the chastity of your soul. You are worthy to have the care of the royal apartments confided to you." Then, turning to the other messenger, he said: "But you, who have such unmortified eyes, depart from the palace. You shall not remain in my house, for I have no confidence in your virtue."[119]

Custody of the eyes was a subject of teaching of many of the saints. For instance St Augustine in his Rule admonished his brethren in these words, "Although your eyes may perhaps fall on a woman, they must never be fixed on her. For in passing here and there, you are not forbidden to see women, but to desire them or wish to be desired by them is wicked. On either side bad passions are stirred up, and that not merely by touch or by thought, but by sight alone. And say not that your minds are pure if your eyes are not kept in modest restraint, for the immodest eye is the messenger of the impure heart. And when such hearts exchange thoughts by looks though without words and by

---

[119] *The Works of the Seraphic Father St Francis of Assisi*, London: R. Washbourne, 1882, pp. 254-255.

fleshly concupiscence allure each other with evil desires, then chastity flies from the soul, even though the body is free from outward stain."[120]

The eyes are a means of communication, or outward action. They are closely connected to the soul. It is often argued that looking can be no harm provided that one does not act on those looks. However, outward actions are signs of inward realties. Looking is simply doing with the eyes what one wishes to do in the soul but still does not. It is conforming to Christian morality on the outside while constantly rebelling on the inside. The eyes, as the saying goes, are the windows to the soul; they expose the inward reality more clearly than any other part of the body. Therefore, failure to keep guard over the eyes is a failure to keep guard over the heart.

Custody of the eyes means that we will avert our eyes when we see something which is in conflict with our pursuit of chastity.

Pornography

In speaking about custody of the eyes we need to give particular attention to the question of pornography as it has reached plague proportions in our society. On Ash Wednesday, 2007, Bishop Robert W. Finn, Bishop of Kansas City, published a pastoral letter entitled, "Blessed are the pure in heart". In it he addressed the reality of the growing problem of addiction to pornography in his own country. He produced some extraordinary statistics on the problem of pornography in the United States. What he depicts would be of similar proportions in Australia.

He reports that in 2004 there were 4.2 million pornographic websites with 372 million pornographic pages. There are 40 million US adults who regularly visit internet pornography websites. 70% of 18 to 24 year old men visit pornographic sites in a typical month. 66% of men in their 20s and 30s also report being regular users of

---

[120] Rule of St Augustine, Chapter 4, On Conduct and Fraternal Correction.

pornography. One out of every six women grapples with addiction to pornography. While pornography is not a new problem for humanity, the development of the mass media has made it much easier to access it anonymously.

The word "pornography" comes from the Greek words, *porne*, meaning a prostitute and *graphos*, meaning a writing or depiction. If we put both words together we arrive at "A depiction or description of the activities of prostitutes." Thus, it can be described as the portrayal of erotic behaviour designed to cause sexual excitement.

The *Catechism of the Catholic Church* says: "Pornography consists in removing real or simulated acts from the intimacy of the partners, in order to display them deliberately to third parties. It offends against chastity because it perverts the conjugal act, the intimate giving of spouses to each other. It does grave injury to the dignity of its participants (actors, vendors, the public), since each one becomes an object of base pleasure and illicit profit for others. It immerses all who are involved in the illusion of a fantasy world. It is a grave offense."[121] The Lord himself teaches in St Matthew's Gospel (5:28): "if a man looks at a woman lustfully, he has already committed adultery with her in his heart." Indeed the biblical warning is severe: "If your eye should be your downfall, tear it out" (*Mark* 9:47).

Access to pornography can quickly become addictive. Psychologists explain that pornography's addictive strength is a result of long-term, sometimes lifelong, neuroplastic changes in the brain. Simply put, pornographic material is potent and addictive and it becomes permanently implanted in the brain. Psychiatrist Norman Doidge, author of the book, *The Brain That Changes Itself,* writes, "Pornography, by offering an endless harem of sexual objects, hyperactivates the appetitive system. Porn viewers develop new maps in their brains, based on the photos and videos they see. Because it is a

---

[121] *Catechism of the Catholic Church*, n. 2354.

use-it-or-lose-it brain, when we develop a map area, we long to keep it activated. Just as our muscles become impatient for exercise if we've been sitting all day, so too do our senses hunger to be stimulated."[122]

Doidge further notes that porn viewers develop a tolerance which means that they need more and more stimulation. Thus, they often move to harder, more deviant pornography. Viewing pornography has the effect of changing the user's attitude toward sex. The user becomes dependent on needing sexual fantasies to get aroused. They can require their partners to act out pornographic scenes. They can get caught up in sexual harassment and sexual aggression. They lose a sense of the real meaning of sex so that it becomes seen as a casual, non-intimate, recreational activity. Those addicted to pornography will find themselves never satisfied. For married people it often becomes a source of marriage tension and can lead to divorce.

Marital love is meant to be a total giving of oneself to a lifelong, faithful partner. It is a trusting, selfless giving. By contrast, pornographic sex is selfish, demeaning and mechanical.

Bishop Finn teaches in his letter: "Pornography perverts the beauty of intimate love proper to marriage, presenting images of the body and sexual acts for base pleasure – regarding other persons as objects to be used, manipulated, and sold".

He says, "Our human sexuality is created as something good by God. It is a gift. It also suffers from the effects of original sin and so can manifest not only good but evil. Pornography is one such evil. It assaults human dignity and commodifies people and human sexuality. It starves the human soul which has a spiritual dimension which must be nurtured by giving and receiving a personal love".

He says further, "Pornography violates modesty, chastity and truth. Human sexuality involves modesty which protects the privacy of individuals regarding what is most personal and intimate. To invade

---

122 Norman Diodge, *The Brain That Changes Itself,* Penguin, 2007.

this privacy, and unveil what should remain hidden, is an assault on human dignity".

In a section entitled, "The bitter fruit of pornography", Bishop Finn speaks of the harm that pornography has not only on the user but on families, on children and on society. We hear the claim that pornography does not hurt anyone. To this he answers, "Within the person, pornography wreaks harm physically, emotionally and spiritually. Pornography can become as physically and chemically addictive as alcohol, drugs or gambling. The graphic images of pornography burn themselves into our sense imagination. The more deeply and frequently this happens, the harder the road to freedom will be."

Pornography, he says, "stunts a person emotionally. Those addicted may withdraw from friends, family and even their own spouses. Pornography leads them into a world of unreality with idealized, unrealistic figures who do not engage one in a truly human manner. As people withdraw, their interpersonal skills and relationships weaken". Engaging in the use of pornography harms others as well. The industry exploits not only women but also, most terribly, children. "To engage in pornography is to support this terrible and scarring exploitation", he says.

For those who are addicted to pornography the hardest thing is to firstly admit that there is a problem. Bishop Finn comments that the first step in solving any problem is to point it out, to name it. He mentions the Twelve Step Spirituality of such groups as Alcoholics Anonymous. The first step on the road to recovery is to admit that in the face of one's addiction one is powerless. He adds, "People do not address problems that they refuse to admit". While the struggle is not acknowledged, it will not be addressed. Sadly, for the regular consumer of pornography, confession and contrition are normally not sufficient in themselves to break from pornography because, like drug abuse, pornography is not just a bad habit — it is often an addiction. A person with an addiction to pornography will often need specialised help.

A spiritual struggle

In the pursuit of the virtue of chastity, the viewing of pornographic material is a most serious issue. Sadly our society uses sexually charged images all the time to sell products and to attract people to the media. Every person trying to live the Christian life will find that this is an area in which they must struggle.

It can be useful to recognise that this is not just a struggle of the will. It is a spiritual struggle primarily. St John has no illusions. He says in his first letter, "Do not love the world or what is in the world. If anyone does love the world, the love of the Father finds no place in him, because everything there is in the world—disordered bodily desires, disordered desires of the eyes, pride in possession—is not from the Father but from the world. And the world, with all its disordered desires, is passing away. But whoever does the will of God remains forever" (*1 John* 2:15-17).

The struggle for the virtue of chastity is a spiritual struggle. The best form of combat is the use of spiritual weapons. As Catholics we have the use of the Sacrament of Penance which not only enables us to receive forgiveness and find new hope in our struggles, but it is also a source of Grace. The humble recognition of our weakness and our turning to God for forgiveness becomes a means by which God comes to our aid. The prophet Isaiah says of the Lord, "my eyes are drawn to the person of humbled and contrite spirit" (*Isaiah* 66:2). God does indeed turn his eyes towards us in mercy as we come before him humbly acknowledging our weakness and need for his help.

For Catholics, devotion to the Blessed Virgin Mary has always been a source of spiritual comfort and support. In the area of chastity she has a special role. She is, after all, the Immaculate Virgin. Seeking the intercession of the Blessed Virgin Mary is a powerful means for support for both men and women in growing in chastity. Traditional prayers directed to our Lady like the *Memorare* are very suitable in this regard.

A Prayer for Purity of Heart

Prayer is a key spiritual source for the nourishing of the virtue of chastity. Humble and consistent prayer is vital for everyone who wishes to become chaste. When we turn to prayer we are no longer fighting alone, dependent on our own strength of character. We are opening ourselves to the God who "wishes that all be saved". God's grace is real and effective.

There are many prayers for chastity which can be utilised. This is one prayer which is attributed to St Thomas Aquinas which may be suitable.

> Dearest Jesus!
>
> I know well that every perfect gift, and above all others that of chastity, depends upon the most powerful assistance of your providence, and that without you a creature can do nothing. Therefore, I pray that you defend, with your grace, the gift of chastity and purity in my soul as well as my body. And if I have ever received through my senses any impression that could stain my chastity and purity, I ask you, who are the supreme Lord of all my powers, to take it from me, so that I may with a clean heart advance in your love and service, offering myself chaste all the days of my life on the most pure altar of your divinity. Amen

7.

The Crowning of the virtues – Love

St John declares, "God is love, and whoever remains in love remains in God and God in him" (*1 John* 4:8, 16). Christianity is a discovery of love – not just the human experience of love but the profound depths and reality of God's love for us. St John emphasises this point when he says, "Love consists in this: it is not we who loved God, but God loved us" (*1 John* 4:10).

In the midst of the bombings of World War II in the northern Italian town of Trent a young woman was huddled in a dark cellar. In the midst of the suffering around her she sought God. And she comments, "God put a question into my heart meant for us all, and with it came the answer: is there an ideal that does not die, that no bomb can destroy, to which we can devote our lives? Yes, there is. That ideal is God. We decided to make God the ideal of our lives. In the midst of war, the fruit of hate, God was manifesting himself to us as love".[123] Thus began a life and a movement dedicated to the promotion of love[124].

We can know love and be able to give love, because we have experienced love and been nourished by love ourselves. Chiara Lubich says, "The human person needs love in every stage and in every situation of his or her existence. Consequently every child who is born also needs love. Children brought up in a loving environment even while being the centre of attention acquire an inner disposition that develops and grows towards a life of communion. And this disposition

---
123 Chiara Lubich, *Essential Writings*, p. 4.
124 Chiara Lubich founded the Focolare movement.

is fundamental for establishing healthy interpersonal relationships with others."[125]

The Christian teaching is at its most sublime when it speaks of love. It reveals who God is and how human life can be all that it is intended to be. St Paul, in a well known passage in his first letter to the Corinthians, reminds us that no matter what we may achieve in life, if we have not love then "we are nothing at all". He further states that all things will pass and only one thing remains – love.[126] Chiara Lubich says, "Each person's discovery of and achieving certainty that he or she has been wanted and is loved by God – not abandoned to chance or blind fate – is the basis for having that psychological stability which gives meaning to life and a purpose to the world".[127] Love is in the end what lasts. God's love is enduring and consistent. We are bathed in that love. As we discover personally the reality of that love, then we find ourselves capable of giving love. The love of God can be mediated through our closest relationships, especially family. We can know what love is through these experiences. We can also discover the love of God more directly and immediately as a special gift of God to us. We can have even just a moment when we discover and know personally that God loves us – God loves me, individually and personally. This experience can be so profound that many mystics are taken up in ecstasy. This is the testimony of Christian history.

The love of God is real and the discovery of it is a transforming experience. Once we have tasted such love then we are impelled to give such love to others. The experience of the love of God cannot be contained. It wells up and overflows into life.

---

125 Chiara Lubich, *Essential Writings*, p. 224.

126 See *1 Corinthians* 13:1-3.

127 Chiara Lubich, *Essential Writings*, p. 226.

Love incarnated

We have mentioned already the striking claim by Pope Benedict that Christian love engages eros. In an address to a symposium on the encyclical he commented, "Today, the word 'love' is so spoiled, worn out and abused that one almost fears to pronounce it. And yet, it is a fundamental word, an expression of the primordial reality. We cannot simply abandon it, but we must take it up again, purify it and bring it to its original splendour so that it can illumine our life and guide it on the right path."[128] The Pope is calling upon us to rediscover love in its true meaning and let it "illumine our lives".

The Pope's emphasis on reclaiming eros highlights that love must not be over-spiritualised or made somehow platonic. The reality is that love is incarnated in human beings who experience its powerful presence in their lives as they are drawn into rich human relationships. The ultimate human experience of love is found and expressed physically in marriage. The eros between husband and wife is set within the context of a covenant of self giving. Here eros is raised to its full richness and meaning. It is translated from being subject to self-seeking passion to being self-giving.

Eros as incarnated human love is love of desire. It is a yearning. It is an ascending love. It is a love that seeks. The human heart yearns for love. This yearning is the powerful drawing force in human relationships. It is the yearning for completion – "It is not right that the man should be alone" says the *Book of Genesis* (*Genesis* 2:18). This yearning is met in the human experience and yet this experience is not fully and finally satisfying. Indeed many will find their human quest for love seriously lacking. Human beings seek a love which is fully and finally satisfying. That love has a source beyond this world. It is where love "was, is, and is to come" – it is the love which is found in God. The love which we receive from God as we pursue this quest

---

[128] *Deus caritas est*, Acts of the World Congress on Charity, 2006, p. 8.

for love is not only eros but agape. It is the "living water" (*John* 4:14) that quenches the thirsty soul. It, too, is the bread of life which will satisfy our hunger so that we will never be hungry again (*John* 6:35).

Mutuality of love

Love is grounded in a mutual receptivity. We give love because we have received love. To be able to give love we must be open to receiving love. Love has a basic mutuality. Love grows on the basis of this mutuality. Jesus teaches, "I have loved you just as the Father has loved me" (*John* 15:9). To grow under the pure love of God one needs to allow oneself to be loved. Pope John Paul II taught, "To imitate and live out the love of Christ is not possible for man by his own strength alone. He becomes capable of this love only by virtue of a gift received."[129]

Love among human beings has a face. It is not desire and passion as primeval forces driving us. Incarnated within the whole person love becomes the true source for joy and human flourishing. As human beings we are neither angels nor beast. We are body *and* soul. As human beings we are to be fully integrated in the bodily and spiritual dimensions of our being. One without the other – attempting to be angelic (somehow "above" our lowly flesh) or allowing ourselves to be animalistic (driven by passion in a self-centred way) denies who we are. It denies our essential dignity as human beings.

The love of God for us has a human face – the face of Jesus of Nazareth. His life and his relationships reveal what the love of God is like. The Gospels reveal one who was fundamentally oriented towards those who were poor and suffering. He was willingly associated with those who were considered outcasts and he was accused of being the "friend of tax collectors and sinners."[130] It was precisely these people

---

129 Pope John Paul II, *Veritatis Splendor*, n. 22.
130 See *Matthew* 11:18-20.

who responded to being loved by him – the penitent woman was so moved that she washed his feet with her tears while the tax collector, Zacchaeus, was inspired when Jesus offered to come to his house that he said that he would repay anyone he unjustly treated four times the amount.[131] Love has incited love. The woman loved much because she was forgiven much, Jesus commented to Simon the Pharisee.[132] What is revealed here is that Jesus incarnated a love which reaches out to those who are "far away" and their experience of being loved becomes the path for their response, and the transformation of their lives.

The one who revealed love – Jesus Christ – is the one who presents to his disciples a "new commandment" – "love one another as I have loved you". Jesus' witness of love is to be the criteria for Christian love. It will not just be the example of love but the personal experience of that love which will inspire the quality of Christian love. Love of one another is intended by Jesus to be the defining quality of the Christians – firstly among themselves and then to others. Love overflows from among the brethren to the neighbour beyond.

Love – the service of the Christian to the world.

If love is the experience of the Christian then love is the service of the Christian to the world. When Jesus was asked what was the greatest commandment he answered "to love God with all your heart, and soul, and mind and strength" and "to love your neighbour as yourself" (*Matthew* 22:37-39). Love cannot just be contained in the relationship between the source and the recipient. Love of its nature must flow over beyond its initiating experience to others outside this experience; hence love of neighbour.

The early Christians met a problem when the Apostles found themselves distracted from their task of preaching by the demands

---

131 See *Luke* 19:1-10.
132 See *Luke* 7:36-50.

of practical charity and so deacons were appointed. "*Diaconia*" is the service of love. Pope Benedict comments, "The social service which they [the deacons] were meant to provide was absolutely concrete yet at the same time it was a spiritual service".[133] Christian *diaconia* is a service to a human being, to some*one*, not merely a provision for the needs of somebody. If charity becomes only a "social service" to be "delivered" by a professional it loses its true nature. Charity must be person-to-person in such a way that it does not become a problem to be solved but is rather a human being encountered. This is the true character of Christian love. Christian love is interpersonal and cannot allow itself to become somehow bureaucratic. Pope Benedict argues in this deeply insightful encyclical that Christian social engagement must not only be motivated by Christian love, but must transmit Christian love.

Pope Benedict in *Deus caritas est* makes the point that the just ordering of society is the responsibility of government. The Christian contributes to this task by offering the insights generated by the inspiration of faith. He goes on to argue that the particular realm of the Christian is that of "caritas", the service of love. He challenges the Marxist critique of Christianity that says that the people don't need charity but justice. The Pope insists that justice and charity should not be seen as competitors. The great danger of the pursuit of justice alone is the breeding of a dehumanised society. He says:

> Love – *caritas* – will always prove necessary, even in the most just society. There is no ordering of the State so just that it can eliminate the need for a service of love. Whoever wants to eliminate love is preparing to eliminate man as such. There will always be suffering that cries out for consolation and help. There will always be loneliness. There will always be situations of material need where help in the form of concrete love of neighbour is indispensable. The State which would provide everything, absorbing everything into itself, would ultimately

---

133 *Deus caritas est*, n. 21.

become a mere bureaucracy incapable of guaranteeing the very thing which the suffering person - every person - needs: namely, loving personal concern.[134]

The Christian having tasted love from its source brings this experience into social action. The Pope rightly warns against reducing charitable work to the provision of services. The Christian in carrying out acts of love shows the face of Christ to the person in need. In the end the greatest need of every person, as the Pope says, is the need for love.

Love drives out fear

Human beings experience fear in one way or another. It can be fear of failure, a fear of being rejected, a fear of punishment. Some people's lives can be consumed by fears. Fear paralyses. Fear diminishes our dignity. Fear causes us to close in on ourselves in a quest for self preservation. It is interesting to note how many times the Lord says to his disciples "Do not be afraid". We see moments when Jesus is aware of the experience of human fear at crucial junctures. Peter was overwhelmed with a sense of his own sinfulness, "Leave me, Lord; I am a sinful man." The Lord responded to Peter, "Do not be afraid" (*Luke* 5:8, 10). During his final discourse to his disciples at the Last Supper, they were understandably filled with anxiety, the Lord said, "Do not be afraid" (*John* 14:27). Particularly it is the word of the risen Christ to Mary Magdalene and his disciples, "Do not be afraid" (*Matthew* 28:5, 10). It is also worth noting that the Lord spoke to Paul in the same way. At Corinth God spoke to him clearly, "Do not be afraid" (*Acts* 18:9), emboldening Paul to minister there for eighteen months despite fierce opposition. Sailing to Rome for his trial his ship encountered a storm, and again God told him, "Do not be afraid, Paul"

---

134 *Deus caritas est*, n. 28.

(*Acts* 27:24). "Do not be afraid" is a refrain that runs throughout the New Testament.

St John comments, "In love there is no room for fear, but perfect love drives out fear, because fear implies punishment and whoever is afraid has not come to perfection in love" (*1 John* 4:18). Love casts out fear. This is profoundly true. Love frees us to do extraordinary things. Love fills us with confidence, hope and purpose. For the Christian this is marked by the realisation that we are "sons of God". St Paul teaches, "for what you received was not the spirit of slavery to bring you back into fear; you received the spirit of adoption, enabling us to cry out, '*Abba*, Father!'" (*Romans* 8:15). God has raised us to the dignity of being his sons and daughters. This is our status and dignity in his sight. The words spoken to Jesus on the occasion of his baptism in the Jordan are words that we can take personally to ourselves because we too have been baptised and have received the Holy Spirit, "You are my Son, the Beloved; my favour rests on you" (*Mark* 1:11).

It is the love of God that has done this. Thus, the Christian can face the challenges of life with this consciousness of his dignity, and the love that surrounds him. This love drives out fear.

Companion virtues – mercy and compassion

The *Book of Exodus* describes God as a God of mercy and compassion.[135] These attributes are other expressions of the love of God. Mercy and compassion flow from a heart that has been touched by love. Thus the Christian will reflect these qualities in his life. St Thomas Aquinas defined the virtue of "mercy" in his *Summa Theologiae* as "the compassion in our hearts for another person's misery, a compassion which drives us to do what we can to help him."[136] For St Thomas this virtue has two aspects: "affective" mercy and "effective" mercy.

---

135 See *Exodus* 33:18-19.
136 *Summa Theologiae* II-II.30.1

Affective mercy is the emotion: the pity we feel for the plight of another. The response we have towards those in need is a compassion in our hearts for them. This should then flow into action through effective mercy. If we merely "sympathize" with the plight of another and "share their pain" without making the best of the opportunities we have to help them, then the virtue of mercy does not abide in us in any significant degree.

St Thomas considered whether mercy is the greatest virtue a person can have. While love of God takes a preeminent place, he recognises that when we consider which of the virtues should govern our relationships with other human beings, it is clear that mercy directed to our neighbour in need is the supreme virtue in human beings.[137]

It is worth noting St Thomas' comments on the place of mercy in the character of God. St Thomas writes: "If we consider a virtue in terms of its possessor, however, we can say that mercy is the greatest of the virtues only if its possessor is himself the greatest of all beings, with no one above him and everyone beneath him."[138] This, of course, is properly true only of God Himself. Thus, mercy is, in that sense, the greatest attribute of God.

Love as the growing of character

Following the path of virtue we have come to its zenith in the cultivation of a heart full of mercy and compassion, inspired by the love of God to love our neighbour. Many will say that love of God and neighbour is the goal of the Christian life. There is no doubt that this is true when one considers the teaching of Jesus and that of the New Testament. It is the higher way.

Becoming a person with these qualities of character does require the impetus that comes from a personal encounter with God who is

---

137 *Summa Theologiae* II-II.30.4
138 *Summa Theologiae* II-II.30.4

love. In the final part of this book we will explore the ways in which we can grow in this personal encounter so that we continue on the path to true Christian character.

It also means that the other virtues – those mentioned to date and others that are described in Christian literature – are sought. One cannot just focus solely on being a person who loves without the discipline of growing in the other virtues.

In the final chapters of this part we will consider firstly the question of the engagement of the Christian in the world. And we will briefly consider some of the fruits that come from growing in Christian character.

8.
Service – engagement with the world

As we have seen, the Christian is oriented towards self giving love. The church over the centuries has given witness to this by its works of love. It is a distinguishing feature of Christianity in its involvement with the world. The vast array of charitable works undertaken in the name of the Church, and the numbers of Catholics who have dedicated their lives to such work, clearly show that the call to self giving love has been embraced by the Church. The Christian adopts the fundamental attitude of service towards the society in which he lives. The virtue of Christian service is deeply embedded in the Gospel teaching of Christ. He himself said that he had not come to be served but to serve and "to give his life for the ransom of many". This is the great ideal for the Christian. As Jesus washed the feet of his disciples at the Last Supper he commented "and you are to do the same".[139] The first and most important witness Christians can offer to society is the witness of service which is inspired by love, Christian love. Diaconia, this service of love, is not just an optional extra for the Christian; it is a fundamental aspect of being Christian.

Role in society

These considerations raise the question of how the Christian should see his role in society. It is clear that the Christian cannot adopt a disengaged stance. The Christian should see that there is a responsibility to be involved. This raises the question of the Christian

---
139 See *John* 13:1-20.

taking a role of responsibility. The beginning of this role is through a positive witness. As Christians we are expected by the Lord to be witnesses in society. This witness means that we must in some way step forward. We must be conscious of setting an example. We should be aware of needing to speak out. The Christian cannot keep faith a private matter.

This is an important issue today as many voices are raised to say that Christians should not impose their morality on others. Sometimes it seems that if a person is known as a serious Christian then he is obliged to leave his Christian beliefs behind when he comes to exercise public office or some role of leadership.

A Christian does not see taking responsibility or exercising vital leadership as imposing himself, but rather sees it as a service that is rendered. Leadership in the Christian context is different from a leadership we can find in the world where people "make their authority felt." The teaching of the Lord is very clear:

> You know that among the gentiles those they call their rulers lord it over them, and their great men make their authority felt. Among you this is not to happen. No; anyone who wants to become great among you must be your servant, and anyone who wants to be first among you must be slave to all. For the Son of man himself came not to be served but to serve, and to give his life as a ransom for many (*Mark* 10:42-45).

This is to be the attitude of the Christian to the exercise of authority and leadership.

The leadership we are speaking of here is not just professional leadership but rather it is a moral leadership. We have something very important to contribute to society today. It is not something that will often be appreciated, but nonetheless it is necessary. The history of the Church has witnessed men and women of faith emerging in their generation as great leaders. They did not exercise authoritative roles in society, but were able to be effective influences for good. An example of this is St Catherine of Siena.[140]

Accepting the responsibility to leadership

Many baulk at the idea of exercising a role of leadership. The Scriptures offer us many examples of people called by God to exercise roles of leadership who feel themselves inadequate for the role. What we notice is that God insists. Consider what was asked of Joshua. The *Book of Joshua* begins with the Lord calling on Joshua to take up the leadership after Moses and lead the people into the Promised Land. The Lord promises to be with Joshua: "As long as you live, no one will be able to resist you; I shall be with you as I was with Moses; I shall not fail you or desert you. Be strong and stand firm, for you are

---

140 Catherine was born in 1347. She was the 24th of 25 children. She took the habit of the Dominican Tertiaries. Catherine dedicated much of her life to helping the ill and the poor, where she took care of them in hospitals or homes. Her activities in Siena attracted a group of followers, both women and men. She began travelling with her followers throughout northern and central Italy advocating reform of the clergy. She encouraged a repentance and renewal done through "the total love for God." She began writing letters to figures in authority as she begged for peace between the republics and principalities of Italy and for the return of the Papacy from Avignon to Rome. She carried on a long correspondence with Pope Gregory XI, also asking him to reform the clergy and the administration of the Papal States. In June of 1376 Catherine went to Avignon herself as ambassador of Florence to make peace with the Papal States, but was unsuccessful. She also tried to convince Pope Gregory XI to return to Rome. She impressed the Pope so much that he returned his administration to Rome in January, 1377. Following Gregory's death and during the Western Schism of 1378 she was an adherent of Pope Urban VI, who summoned her to Rome. She stayed at Pope Urban VI's court and tried to convince nobles and cardinals of his legitimacy. She lived in Rome until her death in 1380, at the age of thirty-three. Pope Paul VI gave her the title of Doctor of the Church in 1970 along with Saint Teresa of Ávila, making them the first women to receive this honour. In 1999, Pope John Paul II made her one of Europe's patron saints.

the man to give this people possession of the land which I swore to their ancestors that I would give them" (*Joshua* 1:5-6). The promise is repeated in verse 9: "Have I not told you: Be strong and stand firm? Be fearless and undaunted, for go where you may, Yahweh your God is with you."

Christians should not allow themselves to become passive. The Lord expects us to let our light shine. We may not feel capable to do this and want to stand back and wait for others. But this may not be the Lord's plan at all. We can ask ourselves: have I taken on the responsibilities that are expected of me? Maybe we find ourselves doubting our ability, and holding back.

One who really doubted himself and his capacity to do what the Lord was asking of him was the prophet Jeremiah. The Lord called Jeremiah in these words: "Before I formed you in the womb I knew you; before you came to birth I consecrated you; I appointed you as prophet to the nations." Jeremiah commented on hearing this: "Ah, ah, ah, Lord Yahweh; you see, I do not know how to speak: I am only a child!" But God was not going to let him back away and so replied: "Do not say, 'I am only a child, for you must go to all to whom I send you and say whatever I command you. Do not be afraid of confronting them, for I am with you to rescue you, Yahweh declares." Then, to confirm his intentions we are told:

> Then Yahweh stretched out his hand and touched my mouth, and Yahweh said to me: 'There! I have put my words into your mouth. Look, today I have set you over the nations and kingdoms, to uproot and to knock down, to destroy and to overthrow, to build and to plant.'[141]

What is very evident here is that God had a plan for Jeremiah. Jeremiah felt completely inadequate, but God did not say – that's alright I won't bother you anymore? Rather God says, do not make

---

141 See *Jeremiah* 1:4-10.

excuses! He is promised that God will be with him and support him in what he is being asked to do.

Maybe we think we are unworthy. We see this in the call of St Peter (*Luke* 5:8-11). After the miraculous catch of fish, Peter is overwhelmed, "Leave me, Lord," Peter finally gasps out, "I am a sinful man." Jesus' response is not to say: "OK. You are not worthy!" No – he says, "Do not be afraid. From now on it is people you will be catching." Again we notice that God does not back down when we protest our unworthiness. God knows this only too well. The New Testament has no hesitation in mentioning the shortcomings of St Peter. He gets things wrong on a number of occasions.[142] The story told by St John of the appearance of the Lord to the disciples by the Sea of Galilee after the Resurrection is particularly significant as it reveals how Jesus viewed Peter following his denials. It is told by St John (*John* 21:15-19). It is a passage worth pondering when we look at the poverty of our own Christian life. Peter, of course, had three times denied the Lord – "I do not know him". It is well worth considering how Jesus treats Peter in the light of his serious failure.

In the service of truth

The Christian's service to the world is not only to be expressed in acts of Christian love, but also involves an active engagement with the world to enable the light of Christian truth to shine on the issues confronting society. Christians are not to hide their light "under a bushel".[143] On 21 November 2002, the Congregation for the Doctrine of the Faith published a *Doctrinal Note on some questions regarding the participation of Catholics in political life*. This note, the Congregation said, is "directed to the Bishops of the Catholic Church

---

[142] Some examples are walking on water (*Matthew* 14:22-33), after profession of faith (*Matthew* 16:13-19) and of course the denial of the Lord (*Matthew* 26:69-75)

[143] *Matthew* 5:15: "No one lights a lamp to put it under a tub; they put it on the lamp-stand where it shines for everyone in the house."

and, in a particular way, to Catholic politicians and all lay members of the faithful called to participate in the political life of democratic societies". In the Note the comment was made:

> By fulfilling their civic duties, "guided by a Christian conscience", in conformity with its values, the lay faithful exercise their proper task of infusing the temporal order with Christian values, all the while respecting the nature and rightful autonomy of that order, and cooperating with other citizens according to their particular competence and responsibility. The consequence of this fundamental teaching of the Second Vatican Council is that "the lay faithful are never to relinquish their participation in 'public life', that is, in the many different economic, social, legislative, administrative and cultural areas, which are intended to promote organically and institutionally the common good". This would include the promotion and defence of goods such as public order and peace, freedom and equality, respect for human life and for the environment, justice and solidarity.[144]

The Note makes the point that this has nothing to do with "confessionalism" or religious intolerance. Sometimes people argue that there is, or should be, a separation of Church and State. As we mentioned before today people argue that Christians should not impose their morality on others. But Christians have a role of contributing to the wellbeing of the State by offering Christian insight into issues and problems. St Paul speaks of shining like stars (*Philippians* 2:15). Jesus spoke of his disciples as being "salt of the earth" (*Matthew* 5:13). And in another parable he described his disciples as being a "leaven in the world" (*Matthew* 13:33). This role is really a role of service to the truth, remembering that "the truth will set you free" (*John* 8:32). Truth is vital for the wellbeing of the social fabric.

The Note commented, "For Catholic moral doctrine, the rightful autonomy of the political or civil sphere from that of religion and the Church – *but not from that of morality* – is a value that has been

---

144 *Doctrinal Note*, n. 1.

attained and recognized by the Catholic Church and belongs to inheritance of contemporary civilization".[145] In the face of criticism the Church receives about speaking out on moral issues, it is worth commenting that tolerance – a "virtue" promoted in a society that seeks to enshrine relativism - is not a Christian virtue. Love, justice, mercy, honesty are the appropriate Christian virtues for public life. In a diverse community, tolerance is an important working principle, but it is never an end itself. Tolerance of grave evil within a society is wrong. Likewise, democratic pluralism does not mean that Catholics should be quiet in public about serious moral issues because of some misguided sense of good and loyal citizens. A healthy democracy requires vigorous moral debate. Real pluralism demands that people of strong beliefs will advance their convictions in the public square – peacefully, legally and respectfully, but energetically and without embarrassment. This is the task of the Catholic.

Great Leaders

What makes leaders great? It is tempting to look at their great accomplishments. This is true. But the truly great leader is one who is humble. The humble leader is one who will not take the glory to himself, but will acknowledge that any achievement is due to the contribution of those around him. A truly humble leader will be prepared to accept all failure as his responsibility. Such a leader has true character.

Saints – Models of Christian Leadership

There are so many examples of great Christian leaders. The place to discover them is in the accounts of the lives of the saints. Saints reveal to us the best examples of true Christian character – a quality of character that has left an enduring mark on people's lives and on the history of the Church. We can do no better than come to know the lives

---

145 *Doctrinal Note*, n. 5.

of saints and allow them to become the source of inspiration as to how we can grow and become not only of good character but become in our own way examples and leaders for others.

Christian leadership is not the exercise of power and authority. It is example and inspiration. People look for role models. We all need examples of what we can become. It is natural to want to follow our heroes. For the Christian, our heroes are the saints. In the life of each saint we can see different aspects of the heights of Christian character. Each saint in their own way will realise the accomplishment of Christian virtue. It is estimated that there are more than 10,000 canonised or beatified Catholic saints. It is easy to find details about particular saints using the internet. As well as the best known – St Francis of Assisi, St Ignatius Loyola, St Mary Mackillop, and many others – learning about one's own name saint and birth day saint is a good practice. Each of us has a patron saint who can be a special source of inspiration.

Litany of the Saints

A Catholic custom has been to invoke the intercession of the saints, asking them to pray for us. This form of prayer is used in the Liturgy at times like Baptism and Ordination. It carries the consciousness of being part of the "Communion of Saints". We have a sense of spiritual kinship with them. They are our "older brothers and sisters" in the faith. They are models and inspiration for us still on the way. We seek their prayer for us. Saying the Litany of the Saints can be a way of uniting our lives with their realisation of Christian virtue.

Lord, have mercy on us.	Lord, have mercy on us.
Christ, have mercy on us.	Christ, have mercy on us.
Lord, have mercy on us.	Lord, have mercy on us.
Christ, hear us.	Christ, graciously hear us.

God, the Father of heaven, have mercy on us.
God the Son, Redeemer of the world, have mercy on us.
God the Holy Spirit, have mercy on us.
Holy Trinity, one God, have mercy on us.

Holy Mary, pray for us.
Holy Mother of God, pray for us.
Holy Virgin of virgins, pray for us.
St Michael, pray for us.
St Gabriel, pray for us.
St Raphael, pray for us.
All you Holy Angels and Archangels, pray for us.
St John the Baptist, pray for us.
St Joseph, pray for us.
All you Holy Patriarchs and Prophets, pray for us.

St Peter,	pray for us.
St Paul,	pray for us.
St Andrew,	pray for us.
St James,	pray for us.
St John,	pray for us.
St Thomas,	pray for us.
St James,	pray for us.
St Philip,	pray for us.
St Bartholomew,	pray for us.
St Matthew,	pray for us.
St Simon,	pray for us.
St Jude,	pray for us.
St Matthias,	pray for us.
St Barnabas,	pray for us.
St Luke,	pray for us.
St Mark,	pray for us.
All you holy Apostles and Evangelists,	pray for us.
All you holy Disciples of the Lord,	pray for us.
All you holy Innocents,	pray for us.
St Stephen,	pray for us.
St Lawrence,	pray for us.
St Vincent,	pray for us.
Sts Fabian and Sebastian,	pray for us.
Sts John and Paul,	pray for us.
Sts Cosmos and Damian,	pray for us.
All you holy Martyrs,	pray for us.

St Sylvester,	pray for us.
St Gregory,	pray for us.
St Ambrose,	pray for us.
St Augustine,	pray for us.
St Jerome,	pray for us.
St Martin,	pray for us.
St Nicholas,	pray for us.
All you holy Bishops and Confessors,	pray for us.
All you holy Doctors,	pray for us.
St Anthony,	pray for us.
St Benedict,	pray for us.
St Bernard,	pray for us.
St Dominic,	pray for us.
St Francis,	pray for us.
All you holy Priests and Levites,	pray for us.
All you holy Monks and Hermits,	pray for us.
St Mary Magdalene,	pray for us.
St Agatha,	pray for us.
St Lucy,	pray for us.
St Agnes,	pray for us.
St Cecilia,	pray for us.
St Anastasia,	pray for us.
St Catherine,	pray for us.
St Clare,	pray for us.
All you holy Virgins and Widows,	pray for us.
All you holy Saints of God,	pray for us.

9.
Hope and Joy – the fruit of Faith

Everyone wants to have a happy life. This universal human longing is faced with many forces that can thwart its realisation. Contemporary society constantly offers recipes for happiness. They vary from pursuit of material goals to esoteric spiritualism. Anything that offers a path to happiness will have some adherents; such is the thirst of the human spirit. But many paths do not produce enduring fruit. There can be some immediate experience of happiness – for example in the use of a drug – but it is not lasting, and in fact the post-experience can be depressive – for example a hangover after binge drinking.

Post Modernism[146] – with its individualism and relativism – is the predominating influence in modern western culture. Along with its scepticism about finding enduring foundations to culture and art, there is the accompanying denial of God. In 1994, the then President of the Czech Republic and renowned playwright Václav Havel expressed the dilemma of postmodernism when he said that it is "where everything is possible and almost nothing is certain."[147] Caught up in these

---

146 Postmodernism is principally an expression of a Western European "disillusionment" following World War II. It is a cultural, intellectual, or artistic movement which rejects any clear central hierarchy or organizing principle. It prefers to live with complexity, contradiction, ambiguity and diversity, embracing a disinterested relativism rather than seeking to identify solid truths.

147 Vaclav Havel, *The Need for Transcendence in the Postmodern World*, speech in Independence Hall, Philadelphia, 4 July1994.

waves of thought that influence modern secular education as well as cultural expression in the arts and music, it is difficult for a person without a strong anchoring in Christian faith not to be swept up in an environment of perception of life that fosters a nihilism.[148] The world becomes dark and ugly. In his great testament to the sacredness and dignity of human life, *Evangelium vitae*, Pope John Paul II captured the effects of such attitudes on human life in these words, "The eclipse of God leads to the eclipse of man."[149] The Pope proposed a culture of life to oppose this growing culture of death.

Life in western countries is generally very good at a material level. The society is ordered and efficient. There are good prospects for employment and people can enjoy a high level of material comfort. There is access to many technological products and opportunities for travel and money to use of enjoyment. Life is good. However there are many shadows in western life that are mysterious on first reading. Why is there such a high level of youth suicide? Why are so many relationships breaking down? Why are there addictions to alcohol, gambling and drugs? Why is there an increase in the incidence of

---

148 Nihilism is a philosophical position that teaches that values do not exist. It is sometimes realized in an existential attitude whereby life is seen to be without meaning, purpose or intrinsic value. Moral nihilists assert that morality does not exist, and subsequently there are no moral values with which to uphold a rule or to logically prefer one action over another. The term can also depict a mood of despair at the pointlessness of life.

149 In *Evangelium vitae*, Pope John Paul II wrote: "The eclipse of the sense of God and of man inevitably leads to a practical materialism, which breeds individualism, utilitarianism and hedonism. Here too we see the permanent validity of the words of the Apostle: 'And since they did not see fit to acknowledge God, God gave them up to a base mind and to improper conduct' (*Romans* 1: 28). The values of being are replaced by those of having. The only goal that counts, is the pursuit of one's own material wellbeing. The so-called quality of life is interpreted primarily or exclusively as economic sufficiency, inordinate consumerism, physical beauty and pleasure, to the neglect of more profound dimensions—interpersonal, spiritual and religious—of existence" (n. 23).

depression? All this suggests that there is a fundamental malaise at the moral and spiritual level in such societies. It is sometimes commented that people in cultures that have very little materially seem happier than people in societies that have material abundance. Despite all the indicators proposing that life can be good, there are these other signs that suggest that all is not well.

Christian Hope

The contemporary First World suffers because there is a loss of hope. This loss of hope is related directly to a loss of a sense of God which gives the perspective of eternity to the present. Pope Benedict XVI, in his wonderfully lucid style, reflected on the virtue of hope in his second encyclical, *Spes Salvi*.[150] He said, "In the sense that we have been given hope, trustworthy hope, by virtue of which we can face our present: the present, even if it is arduous, can be lived and accepted if it leads towards a goal, if we can be sure of this goal, and if it is great enough to justify the effort of the journey."[151] The Christian has a clear goal in life: it is to "see God face to face". The Christian sees a destiny beyond this world. Thus, contending with the present is made in relation to eternity. The Pope adds that Christians "have a future: it is not that they know the details of what awaits them, but they know in general terms that their life will not end in emptiness... The Gospel is not merely a communication of things that can be known; it makes things happen and is life-changing. The dark door of time, of the future, has been thrown open. The one who has hope lives differently; the one who hopes has been granted the gift of a new life."[152]

The Pope is offering a profound insight into the nature of human life. We human beings need something to live for. If we set our goals on material things, or on human relationships alone, then

---
150 Pope Benedict XVI, *Spes Salvi*. Released on 30 November 2007.
151 Pope Benedict XVI, *Spes Salvi*, n. 1.
152 Pope Benedict XVI, *Spes Salvi*, n. 1.

we will not be truly satisfied: when they fail to meet our needs we can find ourselves empty and without hope. Life can so quickly become purposeless. It is Christian faith that opens up the door to the future, as the Pope says. It is the Christian faith that is the source of a hope that continues to inspire purpose and value to life. The Pope notes in the encyclical that Jesus did not bring "a message of social revolution" like Spartacus, "nor was he engaged in a fight for political liberation like Barabbas or Bar-Kochba."[153] What Jesus brought was "something totally different: an encounter with the Lord of all lords, an encounter with the living God and thus an encounter with a hope stronger than the sufferings of slavery, a hope that transforms life and the world from within ... even if external structures remain unchanged." Christ has made us truly free: "We are not slaves of the universe ... of the laws of material causality." We are free because "heaven is not empty," because God is the Lord of the universe, who "in Jesus has revealed himself as Love."[154]

He comments on the false promises of modern scientific, philosophical, and political thought, and then says that we can "say quite simply: man needs God; otherwise he remains without hope." "Man can never be redeemed simply from outside ... man is redeemed by love," an unconditional, absolute love: "Man's great, true hope that holds firm in spite of all disappointments can only be God – God who has loved us and who continues to love us 'to the end,' until all 'is accomplished.'"[155] The Pope offers a beautiful and profound reflection on the way in which human life is given vitality and direction grounded in a hope born from faith.

A Christian has a perspective on life that is distinctive. Christian faith is not something that is a matter of private interior beliefs that are as good as any other. The Christian who embraces their faith to

---

153 *Spes Salvi*, n. 4.

154 *Spes Salvi*, n. 4.

155 *Spes Salvi*, n. 31.

the full becomes a person "fully alive". It is a truth that the Christian experiences the fulfilment of the words of Jesus, "I have come so that they may have life and have it to the full" (*John* 10:10).

A Christian is one who has a hope in his heart. It is a hope that is not diminished by external difficulties. For this reason people can be attracted to Christianity as they see this hope. They ask what is the source of this hope? Thus St Peter urges us to be ready when this question is asked: "Simply proclaim the Lord Christ holy in your hearts, and always have your answer ready for people who ask you the reason for the hope that you have" (*1 Peter* 3:15).

A sense of hope will be the mark of a person truly formed in Christian character.

Christian Joy

One of the remarks often made about the gathering of young people for the World Youth Day in Sydney in July 2008 was that they were so full of joy. The joy of the pilgrims astounded people. It was a challenge for them, in fact. What amazed people was the fact that these pilgrims did not need alcohol or drugs to manufacture this joy. It was genuine and flowed from hearts full of faith. This joy challenged people to look at what Christian faith has to offer. It was perhaps the strongest witness of all to the truth of the Christian message. People could see that it was not put on. It was simple, humble and absolutely real. It was infectious. Bus drivers joined in the singing. Train carriages were caught up with the spirit. It washed over the city. Many people were deeply touched by this unaffected happiness. Joy is an authentic sign of the Kingdom of God. It is one of the fruits of the Spirit listed by St Paul in his *Letter to the Galatians*: "the fruit of the Spirit is love, joy, peace, patience, kindness, goodness, trustfulness, gentleness and self-control" (*Galatians* 5:22).

The *Gospel of St Luke* particularly captures the spirit of joy which characterises the life of a believer. We can note the joy of Mary in her wonderful song of joy – the Magnificat. We notice the joy of Elizabeth in greeting Mary. We see the joy when Simeon blesses the holy family. The theme runs through the Gospel. One sees Jesus expressing his joy at the experiences of his disciples when they go on mission (10:21). One notes that joy results from the lost being found.[156] Forgiveness restores joy. The Gospel describes the joy of the shepherd in winning back the lost.[157] The parable of the lost coin repeats the theme: there is joy in God's saving mercy.

In the parable of the prodigal son, we see the clearest expression of what we could call "Divine Mercy" when the father runs to the boy (15:20). Here, through conversion, one comes under the divine mercy and the result is joy.

Throughout St Luke's Gospel we see Jesus eating with sinners, e.g., Zacchaeus (19:9). St Luke links joy with the experience of salvation: the "good news" of salvation. This salvation, and hence this joy, is offered to all, and gained through conversion of heart. This theme is recognisable in the Zacchaeus story: there is an invitation to dine, there is a banquet, then a conversion, and finally the resultant joy.

We note also the resurrection joy. Firstly it is a disbelieving joy (24:41), which continues on into the *Acts of the Apostles* as the joyful faith of the Apostles and first Christians. The joy of the eschatological banquet has begun.

Joy is trademark of one who can "put on Christ" and lives the fullness of the Christian life. Simply joy is the fruit of growing in Christian character.

---

156 See *Luke* 15.

157 See *Ezekiel* 34:12-16.

Part 3

Holiness of Life

1.

Life in God

As we saw at the outset of this work, the Christian understanding of human life concerns the interaction between three fundamental realities: the creation, the fall and redemption. At the beginning of this work we examined the nature of human beings as we have been created by God. What God created was good. We identify within ourselves a basic yearning for the good. The account of the Fall given in the Book of Genesis reveals the second dimension to human existence of which we are all painfully aware: sin, evil, moral and spiritual darkness. We see within ourselves the damaging effects of giving in to sin, and we witness daily in the world around us the terrible capacity of human beings to wreak harm and suffering on others.

However, Christianity reveals the sublime action of God coming to our aid. The Incarnation reveals the extraordinary fact that God has chosen to enter the human condition, to become "like us in all things but sin".[158] His action would take on a completely unexpected turn when Jesus of Nazareth, Son of God, would accept death, death on a cross for us. Understanding the mystery of the cross is central to understanding the meaning of our Christian faith. Indeed, without understanding and embracing the mystery of the cross we cannot truly advance in the Christian life.

It will be the orienting of our life around the cross that will enable us to enter the path of personal redemption. Though we have reflected already on the significance of the crucifixion, before we explore the paths of spiritual growth, let us take a moment to visit the events of

---

158 See *Hebrew* 4:14.

Good Friday so that we are able to enter deeply into the mystery which lies at the heart of our faith and is "the power of God to save".[159]

Good Friday is the day we commemorate the death of our Lord, Jesus Christ. This commemoration is not just about remembering the passing of a great and holy man. It is about the incomparable act of the Most High God. It is God himself – Jesus Christ, Son of God - who offers himself as a sacrifice on our behalf. It is the Son of God who cries out to his Father, "Father, forgive them; for they do not know what they are doing" (*Luke* 23:34).

These are not words referring to the cruel executioners, but they apply to all of humanity – to each of us. They are words that refer to the sin of mankind – the constant stream of sin, of evil, of hatred, of cruelty, of selfishness, of lack of love. Sin has horribly disfigured the face of man. It has cast a deep wedge between a creature and the Creator. Sin rejects the God who gave life to humanity in a singular act of love. Man turned from honouring the source of life and love and sought a selfish path, a path of destruction.

Good Friday each year is the day that reveals the response of God to the human condition. God chose not to condemn or destroy as his justice might have required, following the rebellion of our First Parents. God chose instead to manifest the ultimate expression of his profound love for every human being. He asked his own Son to offer up his life in an atoning sacrifice.

God in Jesus Christ took on our human condition and, though sinless himself, absorbed to himself the full sin of humanity and in the dying agony of crucifixion cried out, "Father, forgive them". His prayer was heard and "by his wounds we are healed".[160] This act of ultimate self-giving love set humanity free from the price of our sin: death and separation from God.

---

159 See *Romans* 1:16.
160 See *Isaiah* 53:4-5.

It is upon this basis that we can approach our life in God. This is the foundation to living a life whereby God has become the active agent transforming our inner self. Christian character is fashioned not only by the pursuit of virtue but more importantly by combining it with a growing union with God. This final part of the book will briefly examine some basic elements in the spiritual life, or, our life in God. This inner life will fuel the growth in virtue, the growth in Christian character.

A Life of Grace

The Christian life is a life of grace. The concept of grace is a mysterious one for many Catholics. What is grace? When asked this question one young person answered that it is what we say before meals. This answer does highlight that the concept of grace is a foreign notion to many of us. How do we understand the idea of grace?

There are some major figures in Christian history who are known for their emphasis on grace. One is St Paul. St Paul speaks often about grace. He says that we are saved by grace. In his letter to the Ephesians he says, "Because it is by grace that you have been saved, through faith; not by anything of your own, but by a gift from God; not by anything that you done, so that nobody can claim the credit" (*Ephesians* 2:8-9). St Paul emphasises that we are saved by grace and not by works. This teaching may mystify many Catholics. What does St Paul mean? Before we answer this let us consider another great saint and his teaching.

The second figure in Christian history is St Augustine of Hippo who is called the "Doctor of Grace". He wrote on the subject of grace in answer to the teaching of a fourth century British monk named Pelagius. Pelagius emphasized human freedom and will as the key to living the Christian life. In other words, Pelagius believed we could save ourselves by our own effort. St Augustine wrote strongly against this view.

In his Confessions as he reflects on his own life St Augustine says, "All my hope is nothing except in Your great mercy," and then adds in prayerful thanks to God, "it is only by Your grace and mercy that You have melted away the ice of my evil." St Augustine came to understand that God gives us the power to respond to his commands. He says, "You commanded me ... and since you gave me the power, it was so done."[161]

Why do these two towering Christian figures emphasis grace so much?

Their teaching flows from their personal experience. In both instances they attribute their faith to the intervention of God in their life. St Paul met the Lord on the road to Damascus. St Paul had been persecuting the Christians. God intervened and dramatically changed the whole direction of his life. St Paul realised that without God's merciful action he would have gone completely the wrong way. He attributed his faith solely to the mercy of God towards him.

St Augustine had led a very profligate life. While intellectually brilliant he was subject to his sexual passions. They gripped his life. Then one day he heard what he later described as the voice of a child say to him, "take up and read". The book he had before him was the Letter of St Paul to the Romans. Reading the text before him he was converted. In a moment his soul was set free and he came into a living relationship with God. This he clearly knew was not the result of his own effort. He attributed all to God.

Both men realised that God had intervened in their lives. They were the first to acknowledge that their Christian faith was the result of the action of God. This is what grace is. It is the movement of God in our lives.

Many today do not appreciate the importance of grace in the Christian life. We tend to think that we can manage by ourselves. We think we can save ourselves by our own efforts. We say to ourselves: "I will try to lead a good life". This was what Pelagius proposed.

---

161 See *Confessions,* Book 10.

His teaching is still very much alive today. St Paul and St Augustine would say No, we cannot save ourselves. St Paul summed up what the Christian life is in these words: "We are God's work of art" (*Ephesians* 2:10); that is, the good in us is solely the fruit of God's action in our lives. We must co-operate, yes, but the fruit is God's work and not ours.

The theme of grace is the theme of Pentecost. Here we have an account of a dramatic intervention of God. The Apostles experienced the power of God's Holy Spirit coming upon them. From frightened and confused men they rose up in new confidence and boldness. The power of the Holy Spirit put a "fire in their belly". Immediately after the coming of the Holy Spirit, St Peter went to the balcony of the upper room and preached to the assembled crowd: "Men of Jerusalem, I want to tell you about this Jesus of Nazareth whom you crucified. He has risen from the dead. He is both Lord and Christ". He preached with clarity and boldness. St Luke tells us that his listeners were "cut to the heart". The power of the Holy Spirit invested his words so that they penetrated the hearts of his listeners.

The Church was born as an act of grace. The Church continues in every age by an act of grace.

Grace is at work in our lives. It is a little like breathing. We do not often think about the fact that we breathe, but it is vital to our staying alive. So too grace – the Holy Spirit – abides in us and sustains our spiritual life. St Paul said that we cannot even say "Jesus is Lord" without the action of the Holy Spirit (see *1 Corinthians* 12:3). Thus, just because we do not allude to the action of the Holy Spirit it does not mean He is not active within us.

Both saints declare that in the end all is grace. Our efforts are so paltry. We are God's work of art.

The great theologian St Thomas Aquinas comments:

> Now there are five effects of grace in us: of these, the first is to

heal the soul; the second, to desire good; the third, to carry into effect the good proposed; the fourth, to persevere in good; the fifth, to reach glory (*De Natura et Gracia* xxxi).

St Thomas teaches here that grace precedes any good action, enables it to take place and produces the fruit from the action. He, too, is aware that we are totally dependent on grace. Thus, like St Paul and St Augustine, he is aware that grace is everything.

Grace, the action of the Holy Spirit within us, has flowed out upon humanity as a direct result of the death and resurrection of our Lord, Jesus Christ. St John commented, as we noticed earlier, "He was speaking of the Spirit which those who believed in him were to receive; for there was no Spirit as yet because Jesus had not yet been glorified" (*John* 7:39). The sacrificial death of Jesus released the power and life of the Holy Spirit.

The holy monk St Seraphim of Sarov was asked what was the goal of the Christian life.[162] His answer was, "The goal of the Christian life is the acquisition of the Holy Spirit."[163] This simple yet profound answer reveals a key to understanding the Christian life. The Christian grows in character because the Holy Spirit is the active agent. Indeed, the Christian is one who allows the Holy Spirit to become more and more alive and effective within them. The Christian life is the life of Grace.

This will provide a background to what we consider in these final chapters.

---

[162] St Seraphim of Sarov lived in the 19th century and is one of the most renowned Russian monks. He was a mystic and was responsible for communicating the monastic teachings on the spiritual life to lay people. St Seraphim was glorified (canonized) by the Russian Orthodox Church in 1903. The date of his death is his major feast day. Pope John Paul II referred to him as a saint in his book, *Crossing the Threshold of Hope*.

[163] This teaching is found in Conversation of St Seraphim with N.A. Motovilov.

The path of repentance

As we come to understand that God has poured forth his Holy Spirit upon all who believe in and seek to follow Jesus his Son, so we realise there is a great gift available to us. We are drawn to want the presence and work of the Holy Spirit to be effective in our lives. The Holy Spirit is the great gift of God to each of us. The question we can pose is: how can I live more under the influence and guidance of the Holy Spirit?

There is a key to how the Holy Spirit can shape our inner life. The process of acquiring the Holy Spirit follows a particular path, and this path is the path of repentance and conversion. This may surprise us. However, in order to find the way to growth in personal holiness and in enabling the Holy Spirit to become a truly transforming presence in our lives, we need to walk in the way of repentance.

The Christian life is, in fact, a life of ongoing conversion. Conversion is not just a one-off event. There may be a particular moment of personal conversion and this is vital to the radical re-orientation of our lives around faith in Jesus Christ. However, we must continue to move down this path of conversion, opening more and more of our lives to the transforming work of God.

The Lord's key proclamation, "Repent, for the kingdom of Heaven is close at hand" (*Matthew* 3:2) continues as daily call to us. The Christian must walk in this path of conversion, hearing the Gospel challenge us to enter more and more into the way of God. Each day we need to be open to hearing the Lord call us forward. The Letter to the Hebrews calls on the Christian to accept the admonition of the psalmist, "If today you hear his voice, harden not your hearts."[164]

The Christian life, as the Lord said, is not a wide road, but it is a narrow path that we must follow.[165] But we know that it is the path to life. However, walking the path of faith and pursuing a life of virtue

---

164 See *Hebrews* 3:15 which quotes from *Psalm* 95.
165 See *Matthew* 7:14.

are not just matters of a lifetime of dour personal struggle. As we open ourselves to the reality of our need for God and hence for conversion, we discover that there is the mysterious and wonderful presence of God active within us. It truly is a path of life.

The Christian life follows a particular pattern: that of conversion and grace. The result of this is a transformation of our character from within. We discover that it is a work of God and not just the fruit of our own effort. Yes, there is a personal challenge and cost, but more importantly we see God's grace effective within our lives. When St Paul spoke of the "fruits of the Spirit" in his *Letter to the Galatians* (5:22-23) he described poignantly what happens when a person has submitted their lives to God and allowed the Holy Spirit to become their principle of life. They find themselves growing in "love, joy, peace, patience, kindness, goodness and self control". We are saved through the exercise of our faith which enables God to complete his work in us.[166]

The marvel of the Christian life is that we come to see that we are growing in virtue and in the quality of our Christian life, realising that it is the fruit of the work of God within us. It is not something we have had to struggle to produce by our own effort. We are allowing ourselves to be saved. This is the result of our decision to walk this path of faith and conversion, however the fruitfulness is not from us. It is not our work. No. It is work of grace. As St Paul declares we are God's work of art. What a wonderful conception of the process of growing in Christian character. We are being moulded and fashioned

---

166 This is a key understanding that St Paul has of the Christian life. As we quoted earlier, St Paul said: "Because it is by grace that you have been saved, through faith; not by anything of your own, but by a gift from God; not by anything that you have done, so that nobody can claim the credit. We are God's work of art, created in Christ Jesus for the good works which God has already designated to make up our way of life" (*Ephesians* 2:8-10).

by God. We are becoming more like him.

It is in the Sacrament of Baptism that we establish a relationship with God where we find our true identity and dignity. We are literally "born again" by water and the Spirit. We live a new life: a life in the Spirit. We cease to live unspiritual lives, but we begin to live a spiritual life. As the fire of the Spirit intensifies within us we experience the love of God being poured into our hearts.[167] This love wells over into praise and thanksgiving to God and we cry out in joyful wonder: "*Abba*, Father!" (*Romans* 8:15)

We realise an extraordinary truth – we are in fact the sons and daughters of God and not just in name. We have been brought close to God and his presence is transforming us. We no longer stand off in the background and the shadows like strangers or slaves. No. We have been drawn close to God Himself. Although God reigns in glory in heaven we here on earth have in fact been drawn into the inner life of God. For that is what it means to be a son or daughter. It is to share the intimate family life. God has invited us even now into the inner life of the Blessed Trinity.

God who is love wants us to be drawn into a deep relationship with him. He does not want us to know him through some servile fear or being overwhelmed by his greatness so that we shrink back in our own unworthiness. No. He invites us to come to know him intimately. He wants to share his very life with us. Why? Because, as St John constantly said, "God is love" (*1 John* 4:16). Love cannot but reach out and invite a person into a relationship of intimacy. This is what love is. This is what God who is love does for us. God wants us to know him and love him in and through his own Son Jesus Christ through the power of the Holy Spirit.

At his baptism in the Jordan, Jesus heard these words after the

---

[167] See *Romans* 5:5: "... the love of God has been poured into our hearts by the Holy Spirit which has been given to us."

Holy Spirit hovered over him, "You are my Son, the Beloved; my favour rests on you" (*Mark* 1:11). We can receive these same words as expressions of the Father's way of seeing us. We can hear these words being said to us, "You are my beloved son/daughter, my favour rests on you". In this realisation we can cry out with deep faith and profound gratitude, "*Abba*, Father!"

Jesus, as Son, has shown us the way in which we are to pray to His Father and our Father. Indeed we could not be bold enough to say these words, but because this is how Jesus wants us to learn to pray we have the courage to say, "Our Father, who art in heaven".

Whenever we pray we turn to the infinite God and say, "Father". God sees and accepts us as his very own sons and daughters and wants us to relate to him in this way. This may be beyond our comprehension, but this is what God has done.

Growing in the Spirit is growing in repentance

This is how God sees us: God longs to bring us into the fullness of his own life. However, we are sinners. We are fragile and imperfect. We are far from God. In order that the power and love of God can transform us, we must follow the path of growing in a humble and contrite heart and through repentance allow God's grace to purify us and raise us up in holiness of life.

We can explore this question of the link between growth in holiness and repentance by looking at the life and teaching of St Symeon, called the New Theologian. His experience is worth recounting in order to grasp this truth.

Symeon as a young man aged twenty worked in the public service in Constantinople in the early part of the 10th century. He had sought spiritual advice from a wise and holy monk, also named Symeon, from the monastery of Studion near Constantinople. The old monk taught him the practice of saying many times over, "God be merciful to me a sinner". Young Symeon took the advice and after work in his room prayed this prayer every night, sometimes going through the night. One night he had a special experience of God. He describes it using the third person in the following words:

> One day, as he stood and recited "God, have mercy on me a sinner" uttering it with his mind rather than his mouth, suddenly a flood of divine radiance appeared from above and filled the room. ... He saw nothing but light all around him and did not know whether he was standing on the ground.[168]

This experience had a profound effect upon him and shaped his life's journey from this time on. He had had a direct experience of the presence of God and he attributed this to his practice of invoking the mercy of God. He understood that a person must enter the reality of one's sinfulness in a spirit of compunction. He realised that God, moved by such a person, would pour forth his grace upon them. St Symeon was convinced that this grace was real and could be directly experienced. This had been his experience. St Symeon in his teaching contrasted intellectual theology which abounded in the Church at the time with what could be called an "experiential" theology. He expressed what he now realised as essential to Christian life: "The Spirit which has been sent by God to men ... not to the unbelieving, nor to the friends of glory, nor to orators, nor to philosophers, not to those who have studied the works of the Greeks ... but to those who are poor in spirit and in their way of living, to those who are pure of heart and of body."[169]

Pope Benedict, in his reflection on the life of St Symeon, spoke of the importance of entering more deeply into a life in God by taking this path of repentance. He said:

---

168 This description is found in his book *Discourses* (*Disc.* 22.2–4). Pope Benedict XVI spoke of the significance of the spiritual experience of St Simeon in a Wednesday audience, 16 September 2009.

169 See Hymn XXI. 174.

> Symeon focuses his reflection on the presence of the Holy Spirit in those who are baptized and on the awareness they must have of this spiritual reality. Christian life – he stresses – is intimate and personal communion with God; divine grace illumines the believer's heart and leads him to the mystical vision of the Lord. In this line, Symeon the New Theologian insists on the fact that true knowledge of God stems from a journey of interior purification, which begins with conversion of heart, thanks to the strength of faith and love; passes through profound repentance and sincere sorrow for one's sins; and arrives at union with Christ, source of joy and peace, invaded by the light of his presence in us. For Symeon, such an experience of divine grace is not an exceptional gift for some mystics, but the fruit of baptism in the life of every seriously committed faithful.[170]

The Pope then comments, "This holy Eastern monk calls us all to attention to the spiritual life, to the hidden presence of God in us, to honesty of conscience and purification, to conversion of heart, so that the Holy Spirit will be present in us and guide us".

St. Symeon is regarded as one of the greatest mystics of the Eastern Church and his mystical poetry focussed on the gift of the Holy Spirit is a treasure of the Church. His message is an important one. The path to holiness is discovered through walking the path of repentance. The more we can say with utter conviction – and with tears, St Symeon would propose – "God be merciful to me a sinner", the more our heart is laid open and receptive to the transforming power of the Holy Spirit.

Examination of conscience

The Catholic tradition offers us supplementary ways in which this process of personal repentance can be supported. This is important because an awareness of sin is a challenge for many today. One of the issues we all face is a lack of self-reflection by which we are able to see ourselves as we really are. The busyness of life distracts us from

---

170 General audience, 16 September 2009.

examining the living of our lives. We race from one thing to the next and quickly forget what occurred before. Many Catholics struggle to come to term with sin in their lives. We are quick to make excuses for what we know we have done wrong. We can find that our use of the Sacrament of Penance can become fairly routine. The difficulty simply is that we are not able to penetrate far into our conscience in order to see what really needs to be brought to the Sacrament.

There is one age-old Catholic custom which offers a simple antidote for this situation. It is the daily examination of conscience. It is a practice advocated by many of the great saints. For example, St Basil of Caesarea, who developed one of the earliest Rules of Life for monks, instructs them to make an examination of conscience every night. St Augustine in his Rule similarly recommends this practice.

St John Chrysostom comments that as a master requires his steward to give an account of his work day by day, so we too can call ourselves to account every day. St John Climacus puts forward a similar argument in favour of daily examination. He says that as diligent merchants every day make a computation and reckon the losses and gains of that day, so every day we should examine and take account of our losses and gains.

The figure in the Catholic tradition most renowned for encouraging this custom is St Ignatius of Loyola. He states, "Let it be their practice every day to examine their consciences."[171] In fact, he recommended what he called "examen" to be done twice a day. St Ignatius had in mind two kinds of examen, one general and the other particular. The general examen covers all our life (this would be the examen prior to going to Confession). The particular examen concentrates on one fault or sin which is at this moment the particular area which we wish to address. Thus, on a daily basis we are dealing with the call to improve our Christian living. There is much wisdom in this practice. Particular

---

171 Quoted in *Practice of Perfection and Christian Virtues* by Alphonsus Rodriguez.

examen ensures what we could call "sustained motivation" to continue to grow in the Christian life. We know how easy it is to fall away from good intentions. When we track our progress day by day, our capacity to advance is increased.

One particular value in adopting the practice of particular examen is that we can link it to growth in virtue. There may be a virtue that we wish to cultivate. We can make this the focus of our particular examen. For instance, if I want to nourish the virtue of humility, each day I can examine how my conversation, my attitudes and general behaviour mirrored this virtue. When I am able to identify points of failure, I set simple goals to overcome these failures in the coming day.

Thus, incorporating the practice of examen can enable us to make real advances in the growth in Christian character. Of course, examen by itself, while good, is not enough. We have been given a Sacrament which is a powerful means for personal growth in holiness of life – this is the Sacrament of Penance.

Sacrament of Penance

There is a very striking story told by the three Synoptic evangelists of an occasion when a paralytic was lowered down through the roof of a house seeking to be cured of his bodily illness (*Luke* 5:18ff). To the consternation of the scribes present Jesus said, "My child your sins are forgiven". They were quick to point out that only God can forgive sins. They were right of course. Jesus proved that he had this power to forgive by working the cure. This power to forgive sins was entrusted to the apostles after the Resurrection (see *John* 20:22-23). Jesus said: "Whose sins you shall forgive, they are forgiven them". The apostles were to be instruments of God's act of forgiveness not to merely announce God would forgive. This is the ground from which the practice of Confession has grown.

The confession of sins was recommended from earliest times. In one of the earliest Christian texts, the *Didache,* dating about the year

140AD, we meet these words: "On the Lord's day, gather together, break bread and give thanks, after confessing your transgressions so your sacrifice may be pure".[172] St Ambrose speaks of two moments of conversion – one of water and the other of tears – the water of Baptism and the tears of repentance.

Confession of sin to a priest has become a key Catholic practice. In fact the Church requires us to confess our sins once a year.[173]

The Catholic Catechism summarises the development of this sacrament in the Church's history:

> Over the centuries, the concrete form in which the Church has exercised this power received from the Lord has varied considerably. During the first centuries the reconciliation of Christians who had committed particularly grave sins after their Baptism (for example, idolatry, murder, or adultery) was tied to a very rigorous discipline, according to which penitents had to do public penance for their sins, often for years, before receiving reconciliation. To this "order of penitents" (which concerned only certain grave sins), one was only rarely admitted and in certain regions only once in a lifetime. During the seventh century, Irish missionaries, inspired by the Eastern monastic tradition, took to continental Europe the "private" practice of penance, which does not require public and prolonged completion of penitential works before reconciliation with the Church. From that time on, the sacrament has been performed in secret between penitent and priest. This new practice envisioned the possibility of repetition and so opened the way to a regular frequenting of this sacrament. It allowed the forgiveness of grave sins and venial sins to be integrated into one sacramental celebration. In its main lines this is the form of penance that the Church has practiced down to our day.[174]

---

172 *Didache* 14:1.
173 The *Code of Canon Law* gives this requirement as one of the precepts of the Church. See canons 989, 991.
174 *Catechism of the Catholic Church*, n. 1447.

In his post-synodal Apostolic Exhortation, *Reconciliation and Penance* of 1984, Blessed John Paul II addressed the question of the importance of seeking reconciliation with God. Quoting *1 John* 1:8-9 – "If we say we have no sin, we deceive ourselves, and the truth is not in us. If we confess our sins, he is faithful and just and will forgive our sins" – the Pope said, "These inspired words introduce better than any other human expression the theme of sin, which is intimately connected with that of reconciliation. These words present the question of sin in its human dimension: sin as an integral part of the truth about man. But they immediately relate the human dimension to its divine dimension, where sin is countered by the truth of divine love, which is just, generous and faithful, and which reveals itself above all in forgiveness and redemption".[175] Making the regular confession of sins a part of our Christian life helps us to focus on the truth about ourselves. The more regularly we use the Sacrament the more we address the reality of our sinfulness and engage in the process of eliminating sin from our life.

Confession involves more than just the act of confessing one's sins. It includes other elements such as having a genuine sorrow for our sins. It must include a firm purpose of amendment of our lives. The Catholic Catechism teaches: "Christ instituted the Sacrament of Penance for all sinful members of his Church: above all for those who, since Baptism, have fallen into grave sin, and have thus lost their baptismal grace and wounded ecclesial communion. It is to them that the Sacrament of Penance offers a new possibility to convert and to recover the grace of justification. The Fathers of the Church present this sacrament as "the second plank [of salvation] after the shipwreck which is the loss of grace".[176]

---

[175] Pope John Paul II, *Reconciliation and Penance*, n. 13.
[176] *Catechism of the Catholic Church*, n. 1446.

We can summarise the process of reconciliation in this way. Its focus must always be conversion. The first conversion occurred at baptism but we recognise the need for ongoing conversion in growing in the Christian life. The sacrament must be approached with a genuine spirit of contrition. The Introduction to the Rite of Penance states, "The most important act of the penitent is contrition, which is 'heartfelt sorrow and aversion for the sin committed along with the intention of sinning no more'".

The key moment in the sacrament is that of the actual confession of sins. Quoting again from the Introduction to the Rite of Penance, it states: "The Sacrament of Penance includes the confession of sins, which comes from true knowledge of self before God and from contrition for those sins".

The final element to the sacrament is something which is often overlooked – satisfaction. Sin not only affects our relationship with God but often can do wrong to our neighbour. Thus, we may be required to do something to repair the harm; e.g., return stolen goods, restore the reputation of someone slandered, pay compensation for injuries. Simple justice requires this. Sin also affects the sinner himself. While absolution takes away sin, it does not remedy all the damage that sin may have caused. Thus, the Catholic Catechism teaches, "Raised up from sin, the sinner must still recover his full spiritual health by doing something more to make amends for the sin: he must 'make satisfaction for' or 'expiate' his sins. This satisfaction is also called 'penance'".[177]

The Sacrament of Penance is a great tool to facilitate Christian growth. The Church encourages Catholics to use the sacrament frequently. It can also be a great benefit to have a regular confessor.

---

177 *Catechism of the Catholic Church*, n. 1459.

Repentance and the life of grace

St Symeon the New Theologian understood the relationship between repentance and the life of grace. In the call to holiness – "Be holy as your heavenly Father is holy" – the path is that of repentance (see *Matthew* 5:48).[178] The particular means for walking this path is carrying in our hearts the prayer used by St Symeon: "Lord be merciful to me a sinner".

The particular aids to walking this path are a regular use of examination of conscience and use of the Sacrament of Penance.

This path of repentance, St Symeon would assure us, is the path by which we will come to know the power of the grace of God at work in our life.

---

[178] The *New Jerusalem Bible* translates this verse thus: "You must therefore set no bounds to your love, just as your heavenly Father sets none to his."

2.
Prayer

Any person seeking to grow in holiness is aware of the importance of prayer. Prayer is the means by which our relationship with God in Christ can grow. No relationship can grow without communication. So it is with our relationship with God. We need to be in daily communication through prayer.

Relationships are dynamic realities. They are constantly changing. They are either growing stronger or becoming weaker. They never stay the same. What many say about relationships is very true: we need to work at them. Our relationship with God will be nourished as we devote time to prayer – daily conversation with Christ.

Communication is a two way thing. We have to come into a dialogue with Christ, and not just subject him to a monologue. We need to learn how to listen to Him. The way this can happen is learning to listen to the voice of Christ in the Sacred Scriptures.

A relationship needs close personal proximity. We have the most perfect way in which this is able to be achieved through the Holy Eucharist. We receive the risen Lord into our hearts at Holy Communion. We can spend time in personal intimacy by silent prayer of adoration before the Blessed Sacrament.

Our Catholic faith revolves around the quality of our relationship with Christ. This has been a theme in the teaching of Pope Benedict XVI. When asked why he was spending so much of his time writing his monumental work, "Jesus of Nazareth", he replied that he simply wanted people to come to know Jesus better and so come into a personal relationship with him. As he expressed it on one occasion: "we ourselves must be personally involved in an intimate and profound relationship with Jesus".[179]

What Pope Benedict is proposing is the same as the great desire in the heart of the Apostle, St John, who wrote: "Something which has existed since the beginning, which we have heard, which we have seen with our own eyes, which we have watched and touched with our own hands, the Word of life" (*1 John* 1). St John wanted others to know the Lord in the same deeply personal way that he had come to know him.

Is this possible for us? Maybe we think that this is the stuff of saints, and completely beyond us. Yet we can all come to enter and grow in this relationship. We can come to know the Lord in a personal way. To do this we need to spend time with him. We need to be in his company. This is what we do when we pray. It is not just the words we say, but it is the fact that we are spending time with him.

Jesus, Man of Prayer

The Gospels show Jesus as a man with a mission - his life was certainly active and full. One does not have the impression at all of a retiring, meditative personality, but rather one sees a man engrossed in teaching, healing and journeying. Jesus involved his life with others, with fishermen and Pharisees, with soldiers and children, with elders and prostitutes, with the poor and the rich, with Jews, Romans and Samaritans. Jesus was a man who spoke forth boldly, who treasured truth and integrity and was not afraid to challenge the established ways of thinking and acting.

Yet as a man so fully occupied, he was also a man of prayer. Indeed, it is precisely because of his deep prayer life that he was so effectively present in the affairs of men. It was in prayer that his mission was nurtured and directed. In prayer he was refreshed, renewed and encouraged.

---

[179] Pope Benedict XVI, Rome, 4 October 2006.

The fact that he prayed is strongly evidenced in Scripture. St Luke records Jesus being at prayer at each of the vital moments in his life and mission: At his baptism (3:21), the choosing of the twelve (6:12), Peter's profession of faith (9:18), the transfiguration (9:28-29), the giving of the Our Father (11:1) and the agony in the garden (22:41). St Luke emphasises here the essential link between prayer and ministry - that each decisive step is prepared for or precipitated by prayer.

We see references to Jesus' practices of prayer in events like the blessing at the multiplication of loaves (*Matthew* 14:19), the blessing of children (*Matthew* 19:13) and in the seeming pause for prayer at the healing of the deaf mute (*Mark* 7:34). Jesus moves into prayer quite freely and openly on each of these public occasions. Prayer is not restricted to the private realm nor is it so totally personal that he does not share his faith in public situations.

His willingness to pray openly is especially seen in two recorded prayers that he utters. Before the tomb of Lazarus (*John* 11:41) Jesus verbally invokes his Father and when the disciples joyfully return from their missionary endeavours he bursts forth into a prayer of praise (*Luke* 10:21-22).

What is also in evidence from the Gospel records is that Jesus deliberately sought extended periods of prayer. Jesus would retire into the hills to pray. We notice this, for instance, after the miracle of the loaves - he sent his disciples away and dismissed the crowds (*Mark* 6:46). St Luke records that it was an established practice for him (5:16). He would spend extended periods of time alone in prayer, either by rising before dawn in the quiet of the early morning (*Mark* 1:35) or the spending of an entire evening or night in prayer (*Luke* 6:12). The impression is given of prayer alone lasting several hours. The beginning of his public ministry was marked forty days spent in the desert - fasting and praying.

We see another aspect of Jesus' prayer life in the fact that he attended the synagogue. In *Luke* 4:16 we are told that Jesus went to the synagogue on the Sabbath "as he usually did". Jesus would have been thoroughly imbued with the synagogue prayer forms, appreciating the sacred texts of the Torah and the prophets and having a rich knowledge of the psalms. He had a deep respect for the religious traditions of Israel. His anger at seeing the Temple (which he described as his "Father's house") turned from a house of prayer to a den of thieves shows how much he honoured the ways of religious practice of the Jews. No doubt, too, Jesus would have grown up in a household that observed the family based religious customs of Israel. He would have recited the Shema daily. "Listen, Israel, the Lord our God is the one, only Lord ..." (cf. *Deuteronomy* 6:4-5 and *Mark* 12:29).

The Emmaus incident (*Luke* 24:30) suggests the custom of meal blessings which Jesus no doubt practiced. The Last Supper, of course, points to Jesus' observance of the feast of the Passover. Jesus entered fully into the religious life of his people; for, as he said of the Jewish law, he did not come to abolish it, but rather to fulfil it (*Matthew* 5:17).

How Jesus prayed

The fact that Jesus was deeply a man of prayer stands unmistakable before us. Let us now consider the way Jesus prayed. St Matthew (11:25-27) records a simple outburst of spontaneous prayer by Jesus. Several key elements of Jesus' way of praying can be seen here. Firstly we need to note the mode of address Jesus takes: he calls God, "Father". This has often been commented upon as a distinctive characteristic of Jesus' prayer. While the Old Testament has reference to God as Father, nowhere is prayer addressed to God as familiarly as on the lips of Jesus. We need to bear in mind that this is Jesus' own prayer here and the address "Father" reflects Jesus' own relationship. In verse 27, Jesus speaks of his unique relationship with the Father: "No one knows the Son except the Father, just as no one knows the Father except the Son and those to whom the Son chooses to reveal him". This very Johannine flavoured saying reflects his unique relationship with the Father, which is a relationship that he invites others to enter, becoming "sons in the Son". Jesus' experience of his Father at his Baptism (*Luke* 3:22) when he is claimed as "Beloved Son" must have been a decisive event that gave him a distinct confirmation of his own identity. Jesus was first and above all Son of God. This was his deepest identity.

The other significant feature of the brief prayer of Jesus is that it is a spontaneous burst of praise and thanksgiving - "I bless you Father". Like the Old Testament psalms, the prayer begins with an expression of praise and then proceeds to expound reasons for praise. In the parallel passage St Luke describes Jesus as being "filled with joy by the Holy Spirit" (10:21-22). As the prayer itself reveals, Jesus' joy is the fruit of seeing the marvellous workings of his Father, that God's ways and the wisdom far surpass human wisdom, or "learning". Jesus marvels in his Father's ways and rejoices in the blessing that has come upon his disciples. Praise and thanksgiving flow because the hand of God is recognised to be at work among men.

It is worth noting that similar elements are to be found in Jesus' prayer at the tomb of Lazarus (*John* 11:42). Praise, confidence in the Father and total union with him characterise this prayer.

Nowhere is the relationship between Jesus and his Father more thoroughly expressed than in Jesus' passion and death. The prayer of Jesus given here reveals the depth of the union between Father and Son. In *John* 12:27 Jesus says, "Now my soul is troubled. What shall I say: Father, save me from this hour?" Jesus sensing his impending death experiences a deep anguish of spirit. He verbalises his dilemma: what shall my prayer be? What will he ask of his Father – knowing as he expressed at the raising of Lazarus (*John* 11:42) that the Father will heed his prayer. It is natural for any man to pray about his own needs: save me, protect me, do not let me suffer, do not let me die. Jesus makes his prayer: "Father, glorify your name!" Jesus opts not for his own self-preservation but for the fulfilling of the Father's plan.

This is more graphically presented in the synoptic accounts of the agony in the garden. (*Mark* 14:32-42; *Matthew* 26:36-46; *Luke* 22:40-45) We need have no doubt that the anguish is real: "My soul is sorrowful to the point of death" (*Mark* 14:35). Fear and great distress are what the humanity of Jesus experiences – his humanity cries out for life and dreads pain. The key issue though is not the acceptance of pain, but the obedience to his Father's will: "But let it be as you, not I, would have it" (*Mark* 14:36). The *Letter to the Hebrews* states: "... he learnt obedience, Son though he was, through his sufferings" (*Hebrews* 5:9). One could be tempted to reverse the words to read "he learnt suffering through obedience" but the author's intention is to point to the fact that to come to perfect obedience involves a deep inner struggle with much personal anguish. This was the agony in the garden: to hand over oneself totally to God.

This, then, is the greatest prayer of Jesus – "let your will be done, not mine" (*Luke* 22:43). Jesus said earlier: "My food is to do the will of the one who sent me and to complete his work" (*John* 4:34) and now this is being asked totally of him. At the same time, Jesus is not unaware of the full dimensions of what he is doing. He sees the essential paradox of his life: "Anyone who wants to save his life will lose it; but anyone who loses his life ... will find it" (*Matthew* 16:25). Knowing a truth is one thing, living it out is another.

The prayers of Jesus from the Cross reveal the state of his soul and confirm the resolution of the anguish experienced in the garden. St Matthew records Jesus crying out, "'*Eli, eli, lama sabachthani?*' that is, 'My God, my God, why have you forsaken me'" (27:46). The words reflect distress, they are the anguished cry of the just man. Yet, taken as they are from *Psalm* 22, they reflect his faith in final vindication; the cry will be heard and answered. In St Luke's account, Jesus' prayer is one expressing that total surrender wrung from his soul in the garden: "into your hands I commit my spirit" (23:46). The words once again invoke a psalm (31:5) which speaks of the anguish of a just man and his trust in being delivered. In St John's Gospel, Jesus' final words express his realisation that the will of his Father has been carried out to the full: "It is fulfilled." The next words reflect his total handing over, the final surrender is death itself: "and bowing his head he gave up his spirit" (*John* 19:30).

The paschal mystery is the central mystery of our faith and we see in Jesus that physical death and life mirror the deeper struggle of dying to self will in total surrender to the will of God. This is the ultimate mystery of Jesus' life and mission and the ultimate content of his prayers.

When his disciples asked him how to pray, Jesus taught them the Our Father. This prayer which we pray so often can best be understood in the light of the prayer of Jesus himself. When, for instance, we pray "Thy will be done ..." we can immediately link our words to their significance in the life of Jesus himself. The prayer he taught his disciples to pray is a prayer that reflected his own personal prayer. It enriches our own saying of the prayer to understand we are praying it with, and in, Christ. It is his prayer as well as our own. The fact that it begins with "Our" Father suggests that it is the prayer of the Church – of all the disciples – it is not just a private prayer. We pray the Our Father as members of the Body of Christ, the Church.

When we come to consider the role of prayer in our lives as Christians, we can take inspiration from the example of Jesus. Prayer is not just a casual and haphazard thing. It is to be integral to the Christian life. There are set times for prayer. There are occasions that evoke spontaneous prayer. There is the deeper prayer of the heart whereby we wrestle with our own desires and those of God. Prayer is a rich and varied experience for the Christian. It is the lifeblood of our relationship with God.

Lectio Divina

With the example of Jesus to inspire us, let us examine one form of prayer that can help us grow in the practice of prayer. It is called *Lectio Divina*. Many today want to grow in a life of prayer and are uncertain as to where to begin. This method is a good starting point.

Lectio Divina literally means "reading holy things". This method is based on the prayerful reading of Sacred Scripture. It is a method of prayer developed by St Benedict for his monks. However, before examining this method it is important to understand how the Fathers of the Church viewed the reading of Scripture.

A man named Origen who was born around the year 185AD in Alexandria can open up an understanding of this approach to prayer. He loved the Scriptures and devoted his life to studying and teaching them. He said some very important things about how we should approach the Scriptures.

> If anyone ponders over prophetic sayings with all the attention and reverence they deserve, it is certain that in the very act of reading and diligently studying them, his mind and feelings will be touched by a divine breath and he will recognise that the words he is reading are not the utterances of men but the language of God.[180]

For Origen, the Scriptures were the Word of God. He taught that if people approach them in the right way they will hear the voice of God. He encouraged an approach to the Scriptures where one seeks out the hidden "spiritual" meaning of the text. He said, "The truth of

---

[180] Origen's works are extensive. He is regarded as the greatest textual critic in the early Church. He produced the Hexapla (a six column Scripture paralleling different language translations of the Bible). He wrote commentaries of almost every book of the Scriptures. He was also a theologian – in *De principiis* (On First Principles) he articulated one of the first philosophical expositions of Christian doctrine. He has also been regarded as a spiritual master for such works as *An Exhortation to Martyrdom* and *On Prayer*. Many of his Scriptural homilies have survived him.

the Word of God is hidden under the surface of the letter". What he taught was that the way to discover this truth is to read the Scriptures in the same way in which they were written: *in the Spirit*. Listen again to Origen:

> The Scriptures were written under the action of the Spirit of God, and they have, beyond their apparent sense, a certain other sense which eludes most readers. For what is found in it is at one and the same time the figure of certain mysteries and the image of divine realities.

We approach Sacred Scriptures in a different way from any other book we may read. When we go about reading a normal book we apply our mind in order to understand the meaning of what we are reading. We are taught to analyse what we read – we are taught to be critical readers. However, the Scriptures must be approached differently. We do use our minds to understand the text, but we need to listen with our hearts to what God may be saying to us. Simply put: In ordinary reading we apply our minds, in reading Scripture we listen with our hearts.

Origen saw the Scriptures as having a body, soul and spirit. The body was the immediate literal sense intended by the human author of the sacred text. The soul was what the Scriptures say to us about our life. This is what Origen called the moral sense. Finally there is the level of the spirit which conveys divine truth or wisdom which reveals God and speaks to our spirit.

To understand what Origen is saying we can reflect on what happens when someone speaks to us. Of course we listen to their words, but we are also attuned to their deeper and more personal communication with us. We pick up the deeper message behind the words that they speak. So it is with the Scriptures. Every time we open the Sacred Scriptures and read something, we are listening to what God wants to say to us. Every time we read the Scriptures it is a moment when God can speak to us.

The key is: are we listening? Are we attuned to the voice of God? Are our hearts open and attentive? There is a story told in the *First Book of Samuel*. The young boy, Samuel in living in the temple in Jerusalem under the guidance of the priest Eli. One night he hears his name being called. He thinks it is Eli and goes to him. The priests sends him away. Again the voice is heard and again going to Eli and saying, "Here I am, as you called me." On the third occasion the priest realised that it was God calling out to the boy and he advised him to respond to the voice by saying, "Speak, Lord, your servant is listening" (*1 Samuel* 3).

This story is a good lesson for us. In fact it teaches an important lesson. God does speak to us. When God speaks we need to listen. The advice of the priest Eli is useful for us each time we pick up the Scriptures to read them. We, like Samuel, can say: "Speak, Lord, your servant is listening". When we open the Scriptures and have this attitude we will find that something strikes us or moves us. A thought may come to our mind. We may realise something about ourselves. We may find some idea in the text that speaks to our lives. We may find our heart moved in some way. The Word in the Scriptures has come alive. The Scriptures are speaking to us.

Lectio Divina as a method of prayer

The *Lectio Divina* method of prayer in its traditional use by the Benedictine monks involved what could be termed an "active" reading process. The reader usually pronounced the words in a low tone and this resulted in several things which enhanced the impact of the words read. It provided a visual memory of written words; a muscular memory of words pronounced; and an aural memory of words heard. This reading process enabled the word to penetrate the person more fully and increased the ability of the person to engage with the word.

Thus, the way we could describe *Lectio* is that it is a slow meditative reading in search of a personal contact with God. *Lectio* as a meditation method involved a process that the monks called *ruminatio*: a word to describe the way a cow chews the cud. The Benedictine tradition eventually saw four stages in this type of prayer: *lectio* as the actual reading process; *meditatio* as the application of the mind and memory to the text; *oratio* as the prayer that issues forth as a result; and *contemplatio* as the delighting in God which is the "grace" of the method.

This approach to prayer has been encouraged in the Church in recent times. The teaching of the Second Vatican Council has inspired this renewed interest in an ancient practice: "The Church has always venerated the divine Scriptures just as she venerates the body of the Lord, since from the table of both the word of God and of the body of Christ she unceasingly receives and offers to the faithful the bread of life, especially in the sacred Liturgy".[181]

Pope Benedict in his Apostolic Exhortation, *Verbum Domini*, particularly mentioned the value of *lectio divina*. He said, "Devote yourself to the *lectio* of the divine Scriptures; apply yourself to this with perseverance. Do your reading with the intent of believing in and pleasing God ... By applying yourself in this way to *lectio divina*, search diligently and with unshakable trust in God for the meaning of the divine Scriptures, which is hidden in great fullness within".[182]

This ancient practice of the Church has much to offer us today. Our prayer is immeasurably enriched when we come to learn how to listen for the voice of God. Prayer becomes both a speaking and a listening. Indeed, growing in the life of prayer leads a person to be more willing to listen than to speak.

---

181 *Dei Verbum*, n. 21.
182 Pope Benedict XVI, *Verbum Domini*, n. 86.

Contemplating the Face of Christ

In his letter at the turn of the millennia, Blessed John Paul II offered a phrase which is captivating. He urged us to "contemplate the face of Christ".[183] It would be valuable to consider this phrase a little more closely. How can we "contemplate the face of Christ"? Essentially it means that we look upon Christ with love. The face is the icon of the person. Instinctively when we meet a person we gaze at their face. Each face is a unique revelation of the person. To contemplate the face of Christ means that we look upon him with love. Two people deeply in love gaze into each others' eyes. Two people in love are satisfied to be in one another's company. Words are not really necessary in the end. It is sufficient to be with the other. Is this possible for us? Maybe we think that this is the stuff of saints, and beyond us completely.

Our faith in Jesus Christ is more than believing certain things about him. It is coming to know him personally. In the 1987 document, *Catechesi Tradendae*, the task of passing on the faith was described as "to put people not only in touch, but also in communion, in intimacy, with Jesus Christ."[184] This statement declares that the goal of handing on the Christian faith to another is not just to provide information about the faith, but to enable the person to come into a deep personal relationship with Jesus Christ. This relationship is marked by intimacy.

Pope Benedict has spoken in these terms on several occasions: "Christianity is not a new philosophy or new morality. We are Christians only if we encounter Christ... Only in this personal relationship with Christ, only in this encounter with the Risen One do we really become Christians ... Therefore, let us pray to the Lord to enlighten us, so that, in our world, he will grant us the encounter with his presence, and thus give us a lively faith, an open heart, and great charity for

---

[183] In *Novo millennio ineunte*, Pope John Paul II devotes chapter 2 (nn. 16-28) to the notion of contemplating the face of Christ.

[184] Pope John Paul II, *Catechesi Tradendae*, n. 5.

all, capable of renewing the world".[185] On another occasion he said, "Our knowledge of Jesus is in need above all of a living experience: Another person's testimony is certainly important, as in general the whole of our Christian life begins with the proclamation that comes to us from one or several witnesses. But we ourselves must be personally involved in an intimate and profound relationship with Jesus".[186]

In order for any relationship to grow and flourish, time is needed. Thus, for us to grow in our personal relationship with Christ we need to be in his company. We can do this firstly through a full participation at Mass, particularly our prayerful communion with the Lord about receiving him in Holy Communion. It is worth noting the term "Holy Communion." At every Mass we come into a holy communion with the risen Lord. The time after receiving the Lord should be the most prayerful of all moments. We return to our seats and commune at an intimate level with Jesus who is truly present in us.

Time with Jesus can be found obviously through devoting effort to daily personal prayer. The Catholic practice of daily prayer – morning and night prayer – is a valuable exercise to ensure that a day does not pass when we have not given attention to the Lord. How strange it would be if we did not greet those of our family in the morning and in the evening. Thus, it is with the Lord who is with us to the "end of the Age".

One Catholic practice that has experienced a revival in recent times is the practice of Adoration of the Blessed Sacrament. Young people, in particular, are being attracted to this devotion. Time given to adoration of the Blessed Sacrament is time devoted to simple attention to the presence of the Lord. It is a particular way in which we can contemplate the face of Christ. The Encyclical Letter of Pope John Paul II, *Ecclesia de Eucharistia,* invites Catholics to rediscover

---

185 Pope Benedict XVI, Rome, 3 September 2008.
186 Pope Benedict XVI, Rome, 4 October 2006.

a sense of awe in the presence of the Sacrament of the Altar.[187] The encyclical speaks about the value of worship of the Eucharist outside the Mass, that is, of adoration of the Blessed Sacrament. It says: "The worship of the Eucharist outside of the Mass is of inestimable value for the life of the Church".[188]

The Pope offers some interesting insights into the place of Eucharistic Adoration in the life of the Church. The second chapter of the encyclical bears the title: "The Eucharist Builds the Church". Quoting from St Paul's *First Epistle to the Corinthians*,[189] the Pope comments that communion with the Blood and Body of the Risen Lord not only builds the vertical communion with the Risen Lord, but also builds the communion *(koinonia)* between all those communicating with the Lord. Vertical communion builds horizontal communion, while horizontal communion becomes the epiphany of vertical communion. Communion with Christ in the sacrament necessarily becomes communion also with all those who receive him.

In adoration we enter an inner spiritual communion with Jesus which awakens love inside us, the love that directs us to all peoples. And not only through adoration do we find the strength to love. Blessed Mother Teresa of Calcutta used to say: "When I look at the Most Holy Eucharist, I think about the poor, and when I see the poor, I think about the Most Holy Eucharist".

When we allow ourselves to come closer to Jesus we find that every aspect of our being becomes shaped and influenced by him. He is not just an historical figure that we know about and one whose teachings we follow, but in coming to know him as a living person we are drawn to put our full and complete trust in him. Christian faith is a thing of the heart.

---

187 Pope John Paul II, *Ecclesia de Eucharistia*, nn. 5-6.

188 Pope John Paul II, *Ecclesia de Eucharistia*, n. 25.

189 "The cup of blessing that we bless, is it not a communion *(koinonia)* of the body of Christ? Because there is one bread, we who are many are one body, for we all partake of the one bread" (*1 Corinthians* 10:16).

Stages in Prayer

Like any relationship our relationship with God grows and changes. In seeking to understand how our prayer-life can unfold we turn to the teaching of the great St Teresa of Avila.

St Teresa speaks of our relationship with God beginning as vocal prayer. This form of prayer will always have a role to play in our prayer-life. We say set prayers like the Our Father or recite the Rosary. However, prayer will not remain at this level – a person will move on to prayer of the mind and heart, to an interior conversation with God.

There are a variety of ways in which we can develop our interior prayer. We have just spoken of the value of *lectio divina*. This prayer can begin in the mind as we ponder Scriptural texts and as we said it will foster prayer from the heart. Other methods of interior prayer that have been part of our Catholic tradition include the practice of meditation developed by St Ignatius Loyola. St Teresa herself promoted the Ignatian method of mental prayer. These practices help us enter into time of spiritual reflection and quiet listening to the voice of God. From these practices we mould the conduct of our lives as we receive insight and inspiration. Often this prayer is accompanied by a desire to grow in virtue as we come to see the value of spiritual things.

In the early stages of a person's effort to develop a prayer-life it is not unusual to experience moments of joy and blessing. These are special and precious graces that inspire us to pursue the inner journey. They help lead us to the next level: from thinking to loving. It also marks another feature of the growth in prayer – we learn to become less busy and more open to the presence of God. We move from activity to receptivity. We move from being centred on ourselves to being more attentive to God.

St Teresa speaks of what is often called "affective prayer", that is, prayer of the affections or emotions. We find within ourselves a growing presence of affections that move our prayer. Our feeling for

God, our love for Him, becomes the inspiration for our time in prayer. We are re-orienting ourselves. God is becoming more the pure object of our prayer, and our prayer is becoming more and more simple.

Sometimes in order for a person to move to a new level in prayer they experience an incapacity to meditate or reflect. A dryness or difficulty may in fact be the means to set the person free from reliance upon a particular method that they have been employing. This is the beginning of the mystical life. It marks the movement towards an habitual state of silence in prayer. St Teresa speaks of stages of "Dark Night" as key ways in which we are purified in our intentions and so enabled to enter deeper levels of prayer.

A person advances in the ways of prayer by the action of the grace of God at work in them rather that the result of their own efforts. This opens the door to a more intense interior life. While it is very helpful to have a spiritual director to guide the person forward, in fact, it is the Holy Spirit who is now the director of the soul. It is the Spirit who enlightens and purifies. The person has entered a holy place and God has come to take possession of their soul.

The beauty of prayer
From what we have described above we can see that prayer opens the path to an intimacy and communion with God that is wonderfully transforming. Prayer is the vehicle whereby God is able to reveal himself more to us and it is the means by which the grace of the Holy Spirit is more effective within us.

We can sense that we are being transformed by the action of God.

3.
Holiness of Life

One of the well known teachings of the Second Vatican Council is the "universal call to holiness". It is found in the Decree on the Church, *Lumen Gentium*, chapter 5. The teaching simply states that all members of the church are called to live holy lives. In other words the pursuit of holiness is not the arena for the clergy and religious alone. This call to holiness is universal in that it is rooted in the Sacrament of Baptism which configures a person to Jesus Christ and brings each of the baptized into communion with the Blessed Trinity.

Such holiness is not necessarily a withdrawal into monastic seclusion where prayer is central to daily life. It is rather a lifelong process of seeking union with God himself, through the person of Jesus Christ in the normal circumstances of life. Speaking of the role of the believer in the world, *Lumen Gentium* taught: "By their very vocation, they seek the Kingdom of God by engaging in temporal affairs and by ordering them according to the plan of God. They live in the world, that is, in each and in all of the secular professions and occupations."[190]

The Catholic Catechism expresses this teaching in these words:

> Hence the laity, dedicated as they are to Christ and anointed by the Holy Spirit, are marvelously called and prepared, so that even richer fruits of the Spirit may be produced in them. For all their works, prayers, and apostolic undertakings, family and

---

190 *Lumen Gentium*, n. 3.

> married life, daily work, relaxation of mind and body, if they are accomplished in the Spirit - indeed even the hardships of life, if patiently borne - all these become spiritual sacrifices acceptable to God through Jesus Christ. In the celebration of the Eucharist these may most fittingly be offered to the Father along with the body of the Lord. And so, worshiping everywhere by their holy actions, the laity consecrate the world itself to God, everywhere offering worship by the holiness of their lives.[191]

While this was a particular teaching that received much attention it was nothing new in the Church. One of the great apostles of this teaching was St Francis de Sales. His work, *Introduction to the Devout Life*, was a book written for lay people. His ministry centred on the spiritual direction of lay people who wished to pursue a more "devout" life. In his book he argues that there is a unique spirituality associated with each person, subject to the situation of their life. He says, "A different exercise of devotion is required of each – the noble, the artisan, the servant, the prince, the maiden and the wife; and furthermore such practice must be modified according to the strength, the calling, and the duties of each individual."[192] To emphasize his point he says, "It is an error, nay more, a very heresy, to seek to banish the devout life from the soldier's guardroom, the mechanic's workshop, the prince's court, or the domestic hearth. Of course a purely contemplative devotion, such as is specially proper to the religious and monastic life, cannot be practised in these outer vocations, but there are various other kinds of devotion well-suited to lead those whose calling is secular, along the paths of perfection."[193]

Another saint, closer to our own time, St Josemaria Escriva, founder of Opus Dei was also a great apostle of the call to holiness. The core of the spirituality he promoted was finding holiness in everyday life. He said, "There is something holy, something divine, hidden in the

---

191 *Catechism of the Catholic Church*, n. 901.
192 St Francis de Sales, *Introduction to the Devout Life*, chapter 3.
193 St Francis de Sales, *Introduction to the Devout Life*, chapter 3.

most ordinary situations, and it is up to each one of you to discover it. Our ordinary everyday life can be a path to holiness."[194] St Josemaria taught that all work carried out competently and honestly can bring the individual and those around him or her closer to God, sanctifying that very work. He considered that whatever was one's profession or work, it is the love with which the work is done, rather than its public profile, that determines its true value.

He offered a way to holiness that is accessible to all. He taught that "any human activity can become a place of meeting God". At the heart of this teaching is the idea that anyone can become a saint and that sanctity is realised within the concrete realities of life. Holiness is fostered when one is faithful to one's daily responsibilities. He proposed a call to heroic virtue exercised within the circumstances of ordinary life. In one of his meditations he taught: "The ordinary life of a Christian who has faith when he works or rests, when he prays or sleeps, at all times, is a life in which God is always present." This path to holiness would not always be smooth and he spoke often of the presence of the cross of Christ. On this he said, "For one who lives the Christian life, the Cross of Christ is a present reality. We accept the cross as a way of purification, knowing that it will lead us to light, peace and joy."

Holiness in the teaching of the Popes John Paul II and Benedict XVI

The possibility of holiness being a feature of the life of an "ordinary" Catholic was a theme found often in the teaching of Blessed John Paul II. In his Apostolic Letter, *Novo Millennio Ineunte*, his master plan for the Church as it entered the new millennium, he proposed that holiness is not so much a state but a task whereby Christians should strive

---

194 St Josemaria Escriva during the Mass when he preached the homily, "Passionately Loving the World" to thousands gathered on the campus of the University of Navarre, Spain (8 October 1967).

for a full Christian life, imitating Christ, the Son of God. Holiness is accessible.[195] This was an innovative teaching in that most Catholics associated holiness with the lives of remarkable saints. Holiness was considered outside the possibility of average Catholics.

The Pope wished to propose that holiness was possible for all members of the Church. He wanted to promote holiness among "ordinary" Catholics. He commented in this regard: "I thank the Lord that in these years he has enabled me to beatify and canonize a large number of Christians, and among them many lay people who attained holiness in the most ordinary circumstances of life".[196] The Pope then could confidently declare: "The time has come to re-propose wholeheartedly to everyone this high standard of ordinary Christian living: the whole life of the Christian community and of Christian families must lead in this direction".

Jesus declared that holiness was the call for his disciples. He quoted from the Old Testament: "You shall be holy; for I the Lord your God am holy" (*Leviticus* 19:2). Pope John Paul II boldly took up this theme when he spoke to young people about the call to holiness and the vocation to be saints. His message for World Youth Day 2000 in Rome captures this theme: "Young people of every continent, do not be afraid to be the saints of the new millennium! Be contemplative, love prayer; be coherent with your faith and generous in the service of your brothers and sisters, be active members of the Church and builders of peace. To succeed in this demanding project of life, continue to listen to His Word, draw strength from the Sacraments, especially the Eucharist and Penance. The Lord wants you to be intrepid apostles of his Gospel and builders of a new humanity".

Two years later for World Youth Day 2002 in Toronto, Pope John

---

195 See Pope John Paul II, *Novo Millennio Ineunte*, n. 30.
196 See Pope John Paul II, *Novo Millennio Ineunte*, n. 30.

Paul II took up this theme once again: "Just as salt gives flavor to food and light illumines the darkness, so too holiness gives full meaning to life and makes it reflect God's glory. How many saints, especially young saints, can we count in the Church's history! In their love for God their heroic virtues shone before the world, and so they became models of life which the Church has held up for imitation by all ... Through the intercession of this great host of witnesses, may God make you too, dear young people, the saints of the third millennium!"

In announcing the 2005 World Youth Day in Cologne – an event he would not live to see – Pope John Paul II sent a letter to the young people of the world: "Dear young people, the Church needs genuine witnesses for the new evangelization: men and women whose lives have been transformed by meeting with Jesus, men and women who are capable of communicating this experience to others. The Church needs saints. All are called to holiness, and holy people alone can renew humanity. Many have gone before us along this path of Gospel heroism, and I urge you to turn often to them to pray for their intercession."

Attending his first World Youth Day as Pope, Benedict XVI built on his predecessor's repeated invitations to young people and at the great vigil of Cologne's World Youth Day on 20 August 2005, Benedict cried out at Marienfeld: "It is the great multitude of the saints – both known and unknown – in whose lives the Lord has opened up the Gospel before us and turned over the pages; he has done this throughout history and he still does so today. In their lives, as if in a great picture-book, the riches of the Gospel are revealed. They are the shining path which God himself has traced throughout history and is still tracing today."

During his Pontificate, Pope John Paul II proclaimed 1,338 Blessed and 482 Saints. He understood that the Church offers its members outstanding models of holiness and humanity in the lives of saints.

In a world that looks for authentic heroes and heroines, John Paul II presented real heroes and heroines of the faith.

The vision of Blessed Pope John Paul II is inspiring:

> Contemplate and reflect! God created us to share in his very own life; he calls us to be his children, living members of the mystical Body of Christ, luminous temple of the Spirit of Love. He calls us to be his: he wants us all to be saints. Dear young people, may it be your holy ambition to be holy, as He is holy.
>
> You will ask me: but is it possible today to be saints? If we had to rely only on human strength, the undertaking would be truly impossible. You are well aware, in fact, of your successes and your failures; you are aware of the heavy burdens weighing on man, the many dangers which threaten him and the consequences caused by his sins. At times we may be gripped by discouragement and even come to think that it is impossible to change anything either in the world or in ourselves.
>
> Although the journey is difficult, we can do everything in the One who is our Redeemer. Turn then to no one, except Jesus. Do not look elsewhere for that which only He can give you, because "of all the names in the world given to men this is the only one by which we can be saved" (*Acts* 4:12). With Christ, saintliness – the divine plan for every baptized person – becomes possible. Rely on Him; believe in the invincible power of the Gospel and place faith as the foundation of your hope. Jesus walks with you, he renews your heart and strengthens you with the vigour of his Spirit.[197]

The call to holiness issued at the Second Vatican Council echoes today in words addressed to young people in particular. Holiness is possible. Saints are born in every age and all Catholics are called to seek holiness of life.

This call is consistent with the tradition of the Church which has spoken of holiness as the way in which we are being transformed by

---

[197] Message to the Youth of the World, on the occasion of the 15th World Youth Day, 29 June 1999.

the active work of the Holy Spirit given at Baptism. The tradition has spoken of the process of *theosis*.

The Christian life as a *Theosis*

Theosis is a term used in Eastern Christian writings to describe the transformation that occurs in the Christian life. It is also called divinization or deification. It witnesses to the Christian reality – by virtue of our baptism we participate in the divine life of God and we enter a path of inner transformation, the life of Grace. What this word emphasises is that God made us to be like Him and He wants us to become like Him and will ultimately transform us into being like Him.

St John taught: "My dear friends, we are already God's children, but what we shall be in the future has not yet been revealed. We are well aware that when he appears we shall be like him, because we shall see him as he really is" (*1 John* 3:2). St John explores this further when he says, "But to those who did accept him he gave power to become children of God, to those who believed in the name of him who were born not from human stock or human desire or human will but from God himself" (*John* 1:12-13).

St Athanasius boldly professed: "For the Son of God became man, that we might become God". St Irenaeus taught: "The Word became flesh and the Son of God became the Son of Man: so that man, by entering into communion with the Word and thus receiving divine sonship, might become a son of God."[198] Maximus the Confessor wrote, "Let us become the image of the one whole God, bearing nothing earthly in ourselves, so that we may consort with God and become gods, receiving from God our existence as gods."[199]

St Augustine amplified this theme when he said, "Let us applaud and give thanks that we have become not only Christians but Christ

---

198 St Irenaeus, *Adv Haer* III 19,1 Quoted in the *Catechism of Catholic Church*, n. 458.

199 Quoted on page 178, *Philokalia*, Volume II.

himself. Do you understand, my brothers, the grace that God our head has given us? Be filled with wonder and joy—we have become veritable Christs!" St Thomas Aquinas stated: "The Only-begotten Son of God, wanting us to be partakers of his divinity, assumed our human nature so that, having become man, he might make men gods".[200]

This teaching, so clearly enunciated over Christian history, emphasises that the path to holiness is the normal path of the Christian. It further emphasises that it is ultimately not the result of our own efforts, but the triumph of God's grace within us. The notion of *theosis* is about what God can and will do in us. Even now we are being prepared for heaven.

This concept can revolutionise the way we see our Christian life. It can help us see that holiness is not a distant possibility. It is something that is possible because God can make it possible.

A Eucharistic Spirituality

Growth in holiness has a particular centre for every Christian. It is the engagement with the great gift of Christ to us – the gift of himself in the Eucharist. Christian character is fashioned under the influence of Christ. Our "holy" communion with Christ at Mass is a powerful means by which we assume his mind and heart.

The Gospel writers faithfully recount the significance of what Jesus did at the Last Supper. He transformed the ancient Jewish Passover meal into the sacramental encounter with his impending death and resurrection. He would be ending his human existence and would offer a new access to him on the sacramental plane. Bread and wine would become his Body and Blood. As he taught in St John's Gospel: "Whoever eats my flesh and drinks my blood lives in me and I live in that person." (*John* 6:56)

---

200 St Thomas Aquinas, *Summa Theologica* I-II, Q.110 a.4.

At the heart of Catholic faith is the Eucharistic spirituality. We live a sacramental spirituality. This is the intention of Christ. We are human beings who need outward signs to aid us in understanding the action of grace. Christ is really present and his saving work is really effective within us. He fulfils his promise that he would be with us "until the end of time" (see *Matthew* 28:20).

The Holy Eucharist, Vatican II tells us, is "the source and summit of the Christian life."[201] Since the Christian life is essentially a spiritual life, we might say as well that the Eucharist is the "source and summit of Christian spirituality". Every Catholic builds their spiritual life around the encounter with the risen Christ in Holy Communion. At each Mass we unite ourselves with the sacrifice of Christ on Calvary. Our acclamation of faith declares the significance of the death and resurrection of Christ for us. Therefore at every Mass we move the heart of our Christian life. We claim afresh the salvation won for us. Pope John Paul II said, "When the Church celebrates the Eucharist, the memorial of her Lord's death and resurrection, this central event of salvation becomes really present and the work of our redemption is carried out. This sacrifice is so decisive for the salvation of the human race that Jesus Christ offered it and returned to the Father only *after he had left us a means of sharing in it* as if we had been present there. Each member of the faithful can thus take part in it and inexhaustibly gain its fruits. This is the faith from which generations of Christians down the ages have lived. The Church's Magisterium has constantly reaffirmed this faith with joyful gratitude for its inestimable gift".[202]

Our personal moment each Mass is when we receive the Body of Christ in Holy Communion. Christ comes to us. The rich imagery used by the Lord in speaking of the vine and branches emphasises that our personal intimate union with Christ is the true source of our life – "for cut off from me you can do nothing" (*John* 15: 5).

---

201 *Lumen gentium*, n. 11; cf. *Catechism of the Catholic Church*, n. 1324.
202 Pope John Paul II, *Ecclesia in Eucharistia*, n. 11.

Receiving the risen Lord in Holy Communion is the source of our own sanctification and an impetus to take the love of Christ tasted in the Eucharist into the world. As Pope John Paul II said:

> Proclaiming the death of the Lord "until he comes" (*1 Corinthians* 11:26) entails that all who take part in the Eucharist be committed to changing their lives and making them in a certain way completely "Eucharistic". It is this fruit of a transfigured existence and a commitment to transforming the world in accordance with the Gospel which splendidly illustrates the eschatological tension inherent in the celebration of the Eucharist and in the Christian life as a whole: "Come, Lord Jesus!" (*Revelation* 22:20)[203]

A final word on Worship

We are called to be saints. Here on earth we can unite ourselves with the saints in heaven in engaging in the Liturgy of the Church as an act of worship. Understanding the nature of Christian worship helps us orient ourselves towards the final perfection of our characters. What we are to become in the future is foreshadowed as the Church invites us at each Mass to join our voices with the choirs of saints and angels who behold God "face to face".

In the *Book of Revelations*, chapter 4, St John says, "Then, in my vision, I saw a door open in heaven and heard the same voice speaking to me, the voice like a trumpet, saying, 'Come up here: I will show you what is to take place in the future'". "A door opened in heaven." *Revelations*, chapter 4, is a glimpse for the pilgrim of what lies ahead: heaven. And what does he see?

The *Book of Revelations* describes this fantastic visionary experience: "The One who was sitting on the throne ... looked like a diamond and a ruby. There was a rainbow encircling the throne, and this looked like an emerald. Round the throne in a circle were

---

[203] Pope John Paul II, *Ecclesia in Eucharistia*, n. 20.

twenty-four thrones, and on them twenty-four elders sitting, dressed in white robes with golden crowns on their heads. Flashes of lightning were coming from the throne, and the sound of peals of thunder". The glimpse into heaven reveals songs of praise and worship:

> Holy, holy, holy is the Lord God Almighty – the one who always was, who is, and who is still to come.

It describes "the twenty-four elders" who "fall down and worship the one who lives forever and ever". They declare: "You are worthy, our Lord and God, to receive glory and honour and power, for you made the whole universe; by your will, when it did not exist, it was created." We are given a glimpse of the sheer dynamism of heavenly worship. The great cry goes up from the angels: "Holy, holy, holy is the Lord God Almighty".

The *Sanctus* is the oldest formal text of the Mass. Clement of Rome (d.104) mentions it:

> For the Scripture says … Holy, holy, holy Lord of hosts; full is every creature of his glory. And we, led by conscience, gathered together in one place in concord, cry to him continually as from one mouth that we may become sharers in his great and glorious promises.[204]

The "holy, holy" is the cry of the people of God. It is <u>the</u> hymn of the Church. It is our moment of supreme praise and worship. We lift our eyes and our hearts to heaven. We hear the angels sing. We join our voices with theirs. Heaven and earth join together in a united hymn of praise – Holy is the Lord our God.

The Sacred Liturgy as Act of Worship

At every Mass we are invited to join the angels and saints in their hymn of praise and we join in singing the Sanctus. We, on earth, participate

---

[204] St.. Clement of Rome, *Letter to the Corinthians* (*1 Corinthians* 34:6-7).

in the heavenly worship. Our voices as we say in the Preface, "blend with theirs".

The document on the Liturgy from the Second Vatican Council, in article 8, states,

> In the earthly Liturgy we take part in a foretaste of that Heavenly Liturgy which is celebrated in the holy city of Jerusalem toward which we journey as pilgrims, where Christ is sitting at the right hand of God, a Minister of the Holies and of the true Tabernacle; we sing a hymn to the Lord's glory with all the warriors of the heavenly army; venerating the memory of the saints, we hope for some part and fellowship with them; we eagerly await the Saviour, Our Lord Jesus Christ, until He, our Life, shall appear and we too will appear with Him in glory.[205]

Our participation in the Liturgy engages us in a cosmic reality. We are lifted beyond ourselves: beyond our meagre concerns; beyond our physical attachments; beyond our earthly preoccupations. We lift up our eyes. We lift up our hearts. We look to heaven. We see through the window. We behold the glory of the Lord.

The Old Testament, too, gives witness to the spirit of worship. A worship of God offered in the temple. In the Psalms there are a number called Ascent Psalms, like the short and simple *Psalm* 134 that captures the pilgrim's intention and expectation:

> Come, bless the Lord, all you servants of the Lord
> Who stand in the house of the Lord through the long hours of night.
> Lift up your hands toward the sanctuary, and bless the Lord.
> May the Lord who made heaven and earth bless you from Zion.

These were hymns sung by pilgrims ascending Mount Sion in Jerusalem to offer worship in the Temple. These psalms express the yearning to offer worship to God. The pilgrims came to the holy city,

---

[205] Vatican Council II, *Sacrosanctum Concilium*, n. 8.

full of faith and expectation. They just wanted to approach the Holy of Holies. They wanted to lift their hands towards the sanctuary. They wanted to come into the presence of the living God. They travelled from their poor and estranged lives to seek the One who is life.

We Christian pilgrims have been given an opportunity "to worship in spirit and truth" in each Mass. We do not have to travel to Jerusalem or some sacred shrine. Each Mass wherever it is celebrated is a moment in which time is suspended. We are united with heaven. We are one with the saints and angels. We, in the spirit, behold the saints and angels. We have a foretaste of heavenly glory. We worship the Lord.

Yearning for God

Every soul yearns for God: "O God, you are my God, for you I long" (*Psalm* 63). We are all "dry weary lands without water". Our souls yearn for God who is the source of our true life. We are dry and empty without Him. When we come to prayer we can sense our spirits reaching out to the One who is the source of our existence and the One who is the sure foundation to our lives.

As the psalmist says, "I gaze on you in the sanctuary to see your strength and your glory" (*Psalm* 63:2). We penetrate the veil that separates us with longing arrows of love. We know it is true: "your love is better than life". And so we are moved to praise and worship the Lord:

> Holy, holy, holy is the Lord God Almighty – the one who always was, who is, and who is still to come.

Prayer of St Francis de Sales

> Lord, I am yours,
> and I must belong to no one but you.
> My soul is yours,
> and must live only by you.
> My will is yours,

and must love only for you.
I must love you as my first cause,
since I am from you.
I must love you as my end and rest,
since I am for you.
I must love you more than my own being,
since my being subsists by you.
I must love you more than myself,
since I am all yours and all in you.

Amen.

Conclusion

St Augustine used bold images in his preaching. He spoke about the Christian being transformed into the nature of God. He commented once in his preaching: "Love what you do, imitate what you celebrate, and become what you praise."[206] The saint had an insight into what is in fact happening as the Christian enters more deeply into the realisation in his life of the faith he professes. Simply put, St Augustine preached that becoming divine is the essence of Christian redemption.

In this line of thought he is close to the teaching of the Apostle John. Thus, it is not unusual to have him say the following as he comments on the *First Letter of St John*: "Each person is as his love. Do you love the earth? You will be earth. Do you love God? What shall I say? Will you be God? Listen to Scripture, for I dare not say this on my own: You are gods, and sons and daughters of the Most High, all of you."[207] He understands that if a person loves the things of the earth then one becomes merely terrestrial, chained, if you like, to this world, while loving God renders one divine. He boldly says in another place that there are "only two types of lives: earthly or heavenly, animal or spiritual, devilish or deifying."[208]

For St Augustine there is a simple choice – we choose God or we choose the world around us. If we cut ourselves off from the divine the human person inevitably attaches himself to created goods. St Augustine knows from his own experience that a person who opens

---

[206] St Augustine of Hippo, *Sermon* 345.5; PL 46.979.
[207] St Augustine of Hippo, *Ep. Jo.* 2.14.5.
[208] St Augustine of Hippo, *de patientia* 415/17.

his life to God will experience the power of the Holy Spirit lifting him up to the realm of the divine – into the "Kingdom of God" as Jesus taught.

Become who you are

It is in this thought context that St Augustine, in a sermon on the Holy Eucharist, stated: "Behold the mystery of your salvation laid out for you; behold what you are, become what you receive".[209] In other words receiving the Lord in Holy Communion becomes the means by which we able to become what we receive. In another place he commented:

> You are saying "Amen" to what you are: your response is a personal signature, affirming your faith. When you hear "The body of Christ", you reply "Amen." Be a member of Christ's body, then, so that your "Amen" may ring true! ... Be what you see; receive what you are.

As we have noted, the Eucharist is the highpoint of our Christian existence – the summit and source of the Christian life. In the moment of profound personal union with Christ, we are giving expression to the reality of the Christian life – we are being transformed into Christ, becoming who we truly are and are meant to be.

The words of St Augustine tell us something very important – the Christian life is about being inwardly changed by virtue of our union with God in Christ. It is an invitation to accept and embrace a power which is available to us. The Christian life is all about sanctification. This is what God wishes to do in us.

However, it is not enough just to know this truth, it is to cooperate effectively with the work of God in us. The way for this to occur is through our personal desire to grow in our relationship with God and to actively seek to grow in Christian character. The more we identify what makes a Christian, the more we can facilitate the work of God within us.

---

[209] St Augustine of Hippo, *Sermon 57*.

The mature Christian character

In the course of this book we have had a short excursion into the nature of the Christian life. We began by exploring the human reality. We considered the implications of human beings being created by God. What God made was good, as the Book of Genesis declares. Next we explored the reality of the sin of our first parents, our fall from grace. It was the price we paid for the gift of free will. We reflected upon the human condition that we know only too well – the interior struggle with temptation and our propensity to sin. With St Paul, we too can cry out, "Who will save me?"

Then we examined the action of God in Christ, the wonder of the Incarnation but moved quickly to considering the implications of the crucifixion of Christ. The cross has become the "power of God to save". Then finally we explored the significance of the outpouring of the Holy Spirit. Now through faith we live a life in the Spirit.

On the basis of this understanding of Christian anthropology we then moved to look at key virtues appropriate, indeed necessary, for the Christian. Considering a series of virtues enabled us to see what Christian character looks like. Our consideration of the virtues enabled us to dip into the rich resource of teaching found in the Catholic tradition. Indeed, the Church has become the "expert in humanity".[210]

Finally we considered the universal call to holiness. Pursuit of the virtues lays the foundation for the flowering of the spiritual life and the transformation of character so that it is marked by genuine holiness. We saw that holiness is for all in the Church and is discovered within the particular setting of our lives.

Witness to the light

Walking the Christian path in humility and faith means that we will grow in such a character that what we become will be a light amidst the

---

[210] This phrase has been used many times. Pope Paul VI used it when he addressed the United Nations General Assembly in October 1965.

darkness. In his *Letter to the Philippians*, St Paul spoke of Christians shining like stars.[211] A person of Christian character does shine like a star in the midst of the surrounding darkness.

The first act of creation was the formation of light. God said, "Let there be light" (*Genesis* 1:3) and so it was. The creative act of God was to dispel the darkness. St John spoke of Jesus as the light that shines in the darkness (*John* 1:5) and Jesus described himself as the "Light of the World" (*John* 8:12).

The Christian is to be that light to the world in becoming who we are – sons and daughters of God assuming the very character of God himself.

---

211 See *Philippians* 2:15-16.

www.ingramcontent.com/pod-product-compliance
Lightning Source LLC
Chambersburg PA
CBHW032023230426
43671CB00005B/184